10.72

Multicultural Child Care

BILINGUAL EDUCATION AND BILINGUALISM

Series Editor

Professor Colin Baker, *University of Wales, Bangor*

Other Books in the Series

Building Bridges: Multilingual Resources for Children
    MULTILINGUAL RESOURCES FOR CHILDREN PROJECT
Foundations of Bilingual Education and Bilingualism
    COLIN BAKER
A Parents' and Teachers' Guide to Bilingualism
    COLIN BAKER
Policy and Practice in Bilingual Education
    O. GARCÍA and C. BAKER (eds)
Teaching Science to Language Minority Students
    JUDITH W. ROSENTHAL
Working with Bilingual Children
    M.K. VERMA, K.P. CORRIGAN and S. FIRTH (eds)

Other Books of Interest

Coping with Two Cultures
    PAUL A. S. GHUMAN
Equality Matters
    H. CLAIRE, J. MAYBIN and J. SWANN (eds)
Language Diversity Surveys as Agents of Change
    JOE NICHOLAS
Language, Minority Education and Gender
    DAVID CORSON
Making Multicultural Education Work
    STEPHEN MAY
The Step-Tongue: Children's English in Singapore
    ANTHEA FRASER GUPTA
Three Generations – Two Languages – One Family
    LI WEI
The World in a Classroom
    V. EDWARDS and A. REDFERN

Please contact us for the latest book information:
Multilingual Matters Ltd, Frankfurt Lodge, Clevedon Hall,
Victoria Road, Clevedon, Avon, England, BS21 7SJ

BILINGUAL EDUCATION AND BILINGUALISM 9
Series Editor: Colin Baker

Multicultural Child Care

Paul Vedder,
Ellen Bouwer and Trees Pels

MULTILINGUAL MATTERS LTD
Clevedon • Philadelphia • Adelaide

Library of Congress Cataloging in Publication Data

Vedder, Paul
Multicultural Child Care/Paul Vedder, Ellen Bouwer and Trees Pels
Bilingual Education and Bilingualism: 9
1. Multicultural education–Netherlands. 2. Early childhood education–
Netherlands. 3. Child care–Netherlands. 4. Children of minorities–Education
(Early childhood)–Netherlands. 5. Multicultural education–Europe. 6. Early
childhood education–Europe. 7. Child care–Europe. 8. Children of minorities–
Education (Early childhood)–Europe. I. Bouwer, Ellen. II. Pels, Trees. III. Title.
IV. Series.
LC1099.5.N4V43   1996
370.19'6'09492–dc20   95-24251

British Library Cataloguing in Publication Data

A CIP catalogue record for this book is available from the British Library.

ISBN 1-85359-308-7 (hbk)
ISBN 1-85359-307-9 (pbk)

Multilingual Matters Ltd

UK: Frankfurt Lodge, Clevedon Hall, Victoria Road, Clevedon, Avon BS21 7SJ.
USA: 1900 Frost Road, Suite 101, Bristol, PA 19007, USA.
Australia: P.O. Box 6025, 83 Gilles Street, Adelaide, SA 5000, Australia.

Printed and bound in Great Britain by the Cromwell Press.

Contents

Acknowledgements

The initiative for this study was taken by the centre for Science and Research at Leiden University after requests from a variety of coordinating bodies in the field of ECCE (early childhood care and education) in the Netherlands. At first, they simply asked for support in evaluating the implementation and effectiveness of strategies for the recruitment of migrant children and involving migrant parents in nursery and play group activities. Eventually, however, they appeared to have more basic questions: What is MCE (multicultural child care), and what is good or bad practice in MCE? How should MCE proceed? We thank them for being persistent in seeking to clarify the questions and answers, and in asking us to support them. We thank the Bernard van Leer Foundation for urging us to consider the problems from an international perspective. This Foundation supports the improvement of ECCE in countries all over the world.

The study was conducted by a research team at the Centre for Intercultural Pedagogics of Leiden University.

A number of people have contributed to the ideas and findings in this book. First there are all of those centres that were willing to participate, especially the centres that we visited. The staff were simply fantastic in their cooperation and help. We also acknowledge the special contribution and support given by the members of the steering committee: Lotty Eldering, Marja van den Sigtenhorst, Rieke Evegroen and Liesbeth Schreuder. Our gratitude goes to the experts who intensively discussed our ideas and findings with us during a workshop (see Appendix 1). Marijke Hamel helped us with all the logistics of this project, and participated in the data collection. Finally, we want to thank the centre for Science and Research of Leiden University and the Bernard van Leer Foundation for providing funds to conduct the study.

1 Multicultural Education: An Important New Challenge

This book is the result of a study on the quality of multicultural education in institutional early childhood care and education. The focus is on the situation in the Netherlands but, as we shall clarify in the coming chapters, the Dutch situation is in many respects comparable to the situation in other Western countries.

In the last 25 years, the Netherlands, like most European countries, has had to cope with a large influx of immigrant families. There have been several reasons for this influx in the Netherlands (Entzinger & Stijnen, 1990). From the Second World War up to the present, the decolonisation of former overseas colonies motivates families from the former Dutch East Indies (including the Moluccas), New Guinea, Surinam, and the Netherlands Antilles to emigrate to Holland. Currently, these immigrant families form approximately 4% of the total population (CBS, 1992; Ministerie van Justitie, 1994). They all have Dutch nationality. Another five per cent of the total population are first or second generation immigrants, but without Dutch nationality. The largest groups are Turkish (215,000) and Moroccans (170,000). They settled in the Netherlands in the 1960s and 1970s as a foreign workforce who compensated for a labour shortage in Dutch industries. This group increased in size in the 1970s and 1980s and is still increasing due to family reunions, family extensions, and family formation. Furthermore, a small but increasing group of asylum-seekers from all over the world has settled in the Netherlands.

Most migrants and asylum seekers differ from indigenous Dutch people in nationality, race and/or a combination of cultural characteristics, such as language and religion. Most immigrant families have a relatively low socio-economic status, and their educational achievement and status in the labour market is relatively low (Van Langen & Jungbluth, 1990; Van der

1

Zwan & Entzinger, 1994). They live mainly in the four largest cities of Holland: Amsterdam, Rotterdam, The Hague, and Utrecht.

Questioning Quality in Multicultural Education

Generally inquiries into the quality of institutional education are only made when there is doubt that educational institutions adequately prepare their customers, children or adults, for a well-adjusted functioning in society (cf. Lundgren, 1983; Vedder, 1992). This study also is motivated by doubts, although part of these doubts are admittedly more related to high expectations about what institutional early childhood care and education (henceforth ECCE) might accomplish than by information about failing practices. Such positive expectations emerge from an optimistic pedagogical notion that children in their early years are flexible and malleable and that interventions and prevention measures have a good chance of success (Clarke-Steward & Fein, 1983; Eldering & Leseman, 1993). In the Netherlands, political support is growing for interventions at an early age to prevent development and learning problems; and not without cause. Educationists point to schools' disappointing effectiveness. In Western Europe, large numbers of immigrant children have problems with the transition from home to school (Eldering & Kloprogge, 1989). The difference in cognitive, social and emotional demands in the home setting and the limited didactic skills of parents and other family members as regards particular Western educational goals, are seen as decisive contributors to such children's developmental problems (Duyme, 1988; Scarr & Kidd, 1983; Snow, Barnes, Chandler, Goodman & Hemphill, 1991). The concern is that these children fail to become self-supporting members of an increasingly demanding society. Child-care centres are increasingly seen as places where the problems can be ameliorated by special interventions (Lucassen & Köbben, 1992; Pels, 1993). It is hoped that child-care centres prepare children for a successful start at school. This function would be specifically directed towards migrant children (a particularistic function). Child-care centres might have a general function as well, viz. to prepare all children for life in a multicultural society. This function derives from a growing concern about an increase in incidences of discrimination in Dutch society and the seemingly tacit tendency among a growing number of citizens to blame migrants and refugees for all kinds of social and personal problems (Abell, 1991; Dekker & Van Praag, 1990; Vedder, 1993). The accomplishment of both the particularistic and general function would be part of what will be described as multicultural education in ECCE.

Culture

Multicultural education is both a complex, and a blurred concept. It is widely used as an umbrella term referring to varying kinds of educational practices related to the multi-ethnicity of societies. In international literature, 'multi' is sometimes replaced by 'inter', and 'cultural' by 'racial' or 'ethnic'. Sometimes the more specific concept of 'anti-racist' education is preferred (Troyna & Edwards, 1992).

The complexity of the concept of multicultural education corresponds to the complex nature of the concept of culture. For several reasons, culture is a controversial concept (Engbersen, 1994). The first reason is that it is a value laden concept. Generalised statements about culture may have a connotation of high or low, elite or plebeian. Defining problems in terms of culture can easily lead to the phenomenon of blaming the victim. A second reason for the term culture being controversial is its oppositional structure. In the conceptual network in which it functions, it is seemingly easier identified by what is not culture, but nature, ethnicity or social class, than by what it is. The third reason is closely linked to this latter remark. Almost any given definition of culture has been criticised for being incomplete or incorrect (e.g. see Bidney, 1953). Nevertheless, we will try to clarify our notion of culture.

We define culture as (a) a set of values, knowledge and skills that educators or leaders want to convey to persons for whom they feel responsible or who are their subordinates, (b) the style and means that they use for conveying values, knowledge and skills and (c) the distribution of responsibilities for this educational or political process. This definition reduces culture to a notion of social heritage and consequently reduces education to being the reproduction of social heritage. Such a definition, so far, does not capture cultural innovations, e.g. due to creativity or contact between a variety of cultures. Moreover it does not include a concept such as cultural domination. We therefore include (d) innovative elements in our definition so that it captures discontinuity and creativity in the way people cope with survival or self-improvement of their circumstances. In our society, notions of culture and how it affects the lives of people should address matters of social class and gender, two important concepts in studies on the distribution of power (Troyna & Carrington, 1990; Vermeulen, 1992). This is necessary for understanding a phenomenon like cultural domination, that is linked to the construction and control of social relationships.

Culture is group-specific, since the preservers and main transmitters of culture, educators and other leaders, perceive the persons they address as their group. In a sense they impose group membership. Group specificity, however, may also refer to the perception by group members or non-group members of values, knowledge and skills, and the context in which they are being transmitted, as constituting a distinctive achievement or destiny of the group. Both processes, attribution of group membership and claiming it, link culture with groups.

Culture is not the only factor important to human interactions and it is not a factor that can be isolated from other factors. Human behaviour is also influenced by ecological and social-economic variables, by situational context and by psychological and genetic variables unique to the individual. Thus, not only within ethnic groups, but also between and within families, and between situations, people differ in their thoughts and acts regarding human development and education (Bowman, 1991; Epstein, 1978). People from different ethnic groups also share identities as (working) women, parents, peers, for example and they often think and act in situations with different cultural codes simultaneously influencing behaviour (Tennekes, 1990).

In defining contents and strategies for multicultural education, and in conveying these contents to children, it is helpful to reflect on the controversial nature of the concept of culture, on the four elements of culture we identified, and on factors that, apart from culture, influence human development and interpersonal and group relationships.

Defining the Problem

The main question in this study is: How can the quality of multicultural education in ECCE in modern Western societies be improved to contribute to a well or better functioning society? This seems only possible if the growth of diversity of groups in society is combined with effective integration and assimilation strategies in education and in other domains in society (e.g. the labour market). Societies must achieve certain levels of integration and assimilation to survive as a cohesive society guaranteeing all its citizens health, education, a sense of safety, self-worth and efficacy (Lynch, 1986; Van der Zwan & Entzinger, 1994).

Before we can explore the main question we have to engage two other questions:

(1) What is the state of multicultural education in ECCE? and
(2) What should multicultural education in ECCE look like?

The latter question provides a basis for evaluating practices of multicultural education. In our study, we analysed the state of multicultural education in ECCE in the Netherlands. We also studied MCE in some centres for ECCE in eight other European countries. The situation in these countries provides valuable comparisons to the situation in the Netherlands.

What is referred to as multicultural education in ECCE in the Netherlands is mainly a practitioner-created educational practice. In creating this practice, practitioners had derived little or no support from theoretical notions, from educational policies or administrative measures. This complicated our task. We had to take a close look at practices of multicultural education, without actually knowing what were their ideological origins. We chose two kinds of anchors for conceptualising multicultural education in ECCE. We used 1) the notion of general and particularistic functions in ECCE as discussed before, and 2) some models of multicultural education that have been developed by others to describe practices in primary schools (Fase & Van der Berg, 1985; Fase, Cole, Van Paridon & Vlug, 1990). Although the lack of conceptual clarity in primary education is a problem as well, the longer experience in adapting to the new demands of a multicultural society has already led to some provisional models for studying multicultural education. The models describe how schools can respond to changes in the cultural diversification of society. We distinguish four models:

(1) Submersion in mainstream language and culture.
(2) Facilitation of a shift between home and mainstream culture and language.
(3) Changing the mainstream culture of and language use within the school.
(4) Influencing ethnic relationships (varying from mutual understanding on the individual level to prevention of institutional racism).

We now provide a description of these models adapted to the circumstances of early childhood care and education.

Model 1 represents a situation rather typical for many young immigrant children in the Netherlands whose education at home and outside home is culturally quite distinct. No special attempt is made to facilitate the integration of the home and education cultural systems or to facilitate children's transitions between the systems. Wall displays and education materials do not reflect a multicultural and multiracial society. The general idea is 'same goals, same approach and same processes for all children'. In its most brutal form, it concerns the implementation of a rigorous assimilation strategy, completely denying the child's home culture. With regard to language, the centres also use a submersion strategy. In a centre operating within the parameters of this model staff may attempt to deliver good quality education and care for all children. Staff have to be skilful with and sensitive to children. Extra help for immigrant children is given because they have difficulty in understanding and speaking Dutch or because they have developmental problems (like any other child might have, particularly those from a lower socio-economic class). Extra help may take the form of lessons in Dutch as a second language. No special attempts are undertaken to recruit children from immigrant families or to appoint ethnic minority staff. An argument used for justifying this model may be 'they came to the Netherlands, so they have to adapt as quickly as possible'.

Model 2 represents practices entailing new or extra educational tasks. Tasks may refer to the

- facilitation of a shift between cultural systems (e.g. by including elements or symbols from home cultures in the centre's main source culture). This may vary from the adaptation of the room by using culturally adapted wall decorations and using culture specific play materials to curricular changes aimed at integration in the main- stream culture via a language and culture maintenance component.
- prevention of, or compensation for, developmental and learning problems that are deemed to be caused by problems with transition between cultures or by the lack of experience within the mainstream culture. An example is the teaching of Dutch as a second language.

This model is particularistic in that it primarily addresses ethnic minority children, and not all children. No explicit attempt is made to create a new cultural system by combining elements from a variety of systems in Model 2. As with the first model, the eventual goal is the transmission of goals and values typical of mainstream culture. Educational strategies and processes may vary according to children's cultural background.

Centres which represent this model tend to put a special effort into recruiting immigrant children. The presence of Dutch children is not strictly necessary, although their presence might be seen as a condition facilitating Dutch language contact and Dutch language acquisition. Immigrant staff provide another important facilitator. They are important for effective contact with immigrant parents. They know about the parents' and children's culture and are therefore better prepared to help children make a transition. To gain information about children's home culture, contacts with parents will be frequent and relatively intensive.

Model 3 also involves progressive educational tasks. The aim is to work towards cultural enrichment by having children learn from knowledge sources that originate in a variety of cultures. Multilingual education, not just for immigrant children, but for all children, is a case in point (see

Cummins, 1990). The goals of Model 3 are directed inclusively at all children,with culture transformation as the eventual goal. The idea is to include elements from a variety of cultures in a culturally innovative manner and combine these in the creation of cultural innovations. Recruitment aims at locating children from a broad variety of cultures, and employing multicultural staff. An open attitude towards a variety of cultures may be visible and tangible for children in the play materials, books, wall decorations and music instruments. Management and staff invest time in getting to know more about one's own and a variety of other cultures, which is seen as a prerequisite for a broad and sympathetic multicultural approach.

Even with a high percentage of minority children, a 'Model 3' centre will not put emphasis on ethnic and cultural differences between children. They nevertheless respect children's home culture and mother tongue by, for example, allowing or stimulating the use of children's first languages and by using games, songs, dances and books from a variety of cultures. They oppose a language and culture maintenance approach in which children are separated along ethnic lines.

Model 4 refers to a general approach directed at the transmission of notions of mutual understanding, solidarity, respect and the equality of all children irrespective of their physical characteristics and cultural background. The social and emotional climate in a group determines whether children will feel safe and secure, and play and learn. Emphasis is put on friendly social interactions between children. Prevention of prejudice and discrimination among children as well as parents and staff are also high on the agenda. Centres would prefer balanced proportions of children from a variety of cultures in the neighbourhood. They would be less concerned about appointing minority staff, but deem it more important that staff are aware about their own ethnocentrism and ways to avoid or overcome it in contacts with children and parents.

The first model conflicts with Models 2 and 3, whereas the fourth model might be combined with the second or third model. In case the fourth model is not combined with another model, this implies that no attempt is being made to change either the minority or the majority culture but that tolerance between representatives of different cultures is promoted.

Earlier we distinguished two functions of multicultural education: a specific function concerning the prevention of ethnic minority children's learning problems, and a general function geared at good care and education for all children. The specific function is represented in Model 2 and the general function in the other models.

Rephrasing the first question, using the models as a point of departure for finding answers, leads to the following question: Can the state of multicultural education in ECCE in the Netherlands adequately be described by Models 1 to 4 or with a combination of elements from these models?

Our attempt to find answers to the second question 'What should multicultural education in ECCE look like?' was guided by a general notion about what quality in such education entails (Vedder, 1992, 1994).

Quality of education may refer to a variety of processes, characteristics and situations but it essentially refers to what children experience. To be able to distinguish 'good from worse' and 'better from best' experiences, we need to stipulate the goals that educators value. If we don't know what goals are important in education, we can't begin to discuss the quality of education. Goals specify particular products of learning and development that can be brought about by education. In terms of culture, the goals represent knowledge and value domains typical for a culture or for different cultures that are deemed important for the cultural reproduction or innovation. Knowing the important goals is thus a first step towards evaluating the quality of education. The second step is finding out about the extent to, and the manner in which these goals are being achieved, in terms of facilitating or hampering the achievement of other important goals. Good quality education is realised in institutions achieving important goals, whereas bad quality education is realised in institutions which achieve either goals of little importance or negatively valued goals or, although they set important goals, have great difficulty in achieving these goals.

In different cultures, educators hold different values and stress the importance of different goals. This inevitably leads to different definitions of good quality education (Vedder, 1994). This diversity in goals and values, especially in a multicultural society, requires inquiries into the quality of education to include the exploration of the social backing of particular goals and values. This is achieved by analysing the explicit or tacit consensus between educators about educational goals and values.

In seeking an answer to the question 'What should multicultural education in ECCE look like?' we make an important premise. The quality of multicultural education in ECCE can't be seen apart from the general quality of ECCE. We shall clarify this by giving a short impression from some of our visits. We were in centres giving a lot of attention to immigrant parents, first language teaching and other elements that are deemed important for multicultural education, but where children seemed to feel lost between the adults, or where the lack of a structured program and the 'child centred' approach of the staff led to chaos, or where the educators' conviction that the centre should compensate for children's lack of opportunity at home to run and jump, justified that 50% of the time children ran around, screaming at, and sometimes kicking each other, and where staff members said things like: 'You see, they really need it'. Such examples clarify that, for the sake of good practice, one should evaluate the total quality of the totality care and education in child centres, of which the multicultural approach is just one aspect.

The Book's Contents

The structure of this book is as follows. Chapters 2 to 4 provide descriptions of practices in multicultural education. Chapter 2 gives a description of the past and present situation of institutional child care in the Netherlands. We pay special attention to multicultural education and studies that others have conducted in this domain. Chapter 3 reports our study on multicultural education in ECCE in the Netherlands. Our attempt to answer the main question, concerning the improvement of multicultural education in ECCE clearly goes beyond the Dutch borders and the outcome is valuable for the situation of multicultural education in ECCE in other (Western) countries as well. We clarify this explicitly in Chapter 4, which presents case studies of child-care centres we visited in eight European countries: Germany, Scotland, England, Sweden, Denmark, France, Belgium, and Spain. The obtained information clearly shows the comparability of the situation in ECCE and multicultural education in ECCE institutions in these countries and the Netherlands. It also clarifies the way centres operate in the different countries and how this is influenced by the countries' particular educational history, traditions and local contexts.

Chapters 2 to 4 contain the information necessary for answering the question: What is multicultural education in ECCE? Chapter 5 gives an analysis of the practices described in Chapter 3 in terms of the four models for multicultural education presented in the preceding section. It clarifies how these models can be used to evaluate practices of multicultural education. The question, 'What should multicultural education in ECCE look like?' is answered in Chapter 6 from three different perspectives: centre staffs', parents' and scientists'.

A central notion in this book is that education in nurseries and playgroups is the mutual responsibility of primary caregivers, most parents and centre staff. We could have paid equal attention to both groups of educators in this study. However, we paid far more attention to the caregivers' perspective than to that of parents'. For budgetary reasons, we could not interview parents and visit children's homes. In Chapter 6, we try to compensate for this by presenting and discussing findings from a study with parents conducted by other researchers.

Chapter 7 contains a presentation of a strategic model, which suggests what should be done to plan and implement changes in ECCE and multicultural education. In the final chapter, we draw conclusions and formulate recommendations and address the main question: How can multicultural education be improved in ECCE?

Throughout this book, we discuss early childhood care and education. Other researchers sometimes use slightly different names for more or less the same phenomenon: e.g. early childhood care and development or early child care.

2 Institutional Child Care and Multicultural Education in the Netherlands: Past and Present

In this chapter we give a short presentation of the past and present of institutional early child care in the Netherlands. This will provide a context for a better understanding of the description of multicultural education in ECCE in the Netherlands in the next chapter.

History

Institutional child care in the Netherlands is not a recent phenomenon. In the 19th century, some form of child care for young children was already provided (Clerkx & Van IJzendoorn, 1992; Singer, 1992). Young children from disadvantaged backgrounds were cared for in infant schools ('bewaarscholen'). These infant schools were initiated by members of the bourgeoisie, and one of the main purposes was to socialise and civilise the children of the poor.

After 1870, another form of child care was introduced, namely nurseries ('bewaar-plaatsen'). The nurseries were open for poor young children (babies and toddlers) whose mothers had to work to earn a living. The children received relatively good care from nurses from the same social background as the children. These nurseries were controlled by a board of bourgeois ladies.

The infant schools largely focused on disciplining the children. In the nurseries, attention was paid to good child care, although the nurses also engaged in occasional playing with the children. At the turn of the century, a new movement lead by pedagogues such as Fröbel arose in Europe. These

11

pedagogues rejected the mere docility training of children, and argued that they learn best through being active. Their focus was on offering sensory-motor experiences and a place where children could play and be stimulated in their social and emotional development supported by sensitive and responsive educators (Skolnick, 1973). These pedagogues started kindergartens. Not until the beginning of the 20th century were these kindergartens ('kleuterscholen') accepted by middle class parents. After the Second World War there arose a popular expansion of kindergartens. Most of the former infant schools were changed into kindergartens. After state legislation was passed in 1957, the opening hours were reduced, and the admission age was raised from three to four years. Kindergartens were primarily concerned with education and less with child care. They were seen as important in preparing children for primary school. Such education in kindergartens was available to all four- and five-year-old children.

In the 1960s there developed women's protests against the traditional distribution of educational responsibilities in Western cultures, which made them primarily and exclusively homemakers and mothers. The protests of these mostly well-educated women soon started to have some effect. These women wanted some free time to follow their careers. To accommodate them a new form of child care for two- and three-year-olds was started: namely the playgroups ('peuterspeelzalen'). They were open for two to three hours, mostly in the morning, for two days a week. Initially, these playgroups were managed by the women themselves, but as the interest grew and more playgroups were started, management was taken over by professional staff, and the focus shifted from childminding to development enrichment. In the 1980s, the growth in the number of such playgroups came to a halt.

In the 1970s and 1980s, the need for full-time day care increased parallel to the growth of the number of women participating in the labour market. Until then, nursery places had still been scarce, and not open for all children. Actions for full-time day care for all children by the women's movement had little effect, because governmental opinion was opposed to places where children were raised by educators rather than by their parents. Not until 1990 did the Dutch government take budgetary action to meet the demand for nurseries. Some 130 million Dutch guilders were then invested every year to increase the number of nurseries (Stimuleringsmaatregel Kinderopvang) (SGBO, 1991). The implementation of this measure is the responsibility of the local authorities.

The Present Situation

At present, the most important child-care centres for children between birth and four are nurseries and playgroups.[1] The present characteristics of playgroups and nurseries result from their specific histories. Nurseries cater for parents' needs for care and education while they are working. Most children attend whole days for at least two days a week. Playgroups were, and are seen more as a relief to parents for just a few hours a few days a week. The motivation among parents for playgroups has however recently shifted. The movement has been from relief more to children's need for or pleasure in playing with peers.

There is no national legislation to dictate a child-care centre's practice or policy. Such are the responsibility of a centre's own administration and local authorities. Each municipality can formulate its own policy on child-care centres, although the association of Dutch municipalities (henceforth VNG; VNG, 1991) has drafted a set of rules that may be used by local authorities.

According to the VNG, a nursery is a centre intended for pre-school children (two months to four years old), mostly open five days a week, for a minimum of nine hours a day. The Netherlands contains three types of nurseries: regular nurseries, company creches, and commercial nurseries. The regular nurseries are largely subsidised by local authority. Parents contribute proportionally to their income. Since subsidies are decreasing, regular nurseries have to sell some of their places to companies (i.e. places for children of company employees). The subsidised nurseries are expected to utilise at least two qualified caregivers per group. The group size ranges from eight to 16 children, dependent on their age. Company creches are financed by the companies themselves and open to children of company staff. Commercial nurseries are often run by national boards. Parents have to cover all costs. No studies are available comparing these different types of nurseries on aspects such as pedagogical approach, staff–child ratio, curriculum and play materials. However, our impression is that differences between nurseries are not related to type but to other characteristics (staff quality and experience, local rules for housing and maintenance, etc.). A recent development in regular nurseries (the growing need to sell places to companies in order to cover costs) means that it is difficult for low-income, non-employed parents to obtain access to a nursery. It is similarly difficult for parents employed in companies that didn't buy places to gain such nursery access.

A playgroup is for children aged 2 (or 1) to 4. They are open for a few days a week, two or three hours a day. Some playgroups are part of a community centre or a centre for adult education. Others work independently. Those playgroups linked with a centre are obliged to work with at least one qualified caregiver per group. The association of Dutch municipalities proposed that playgroups should have the same staff–children ratio as nurseries: one qualified caregiver for each of the following : eight 0–1-year-olds, ten 1–2-year-olds, for twelve 2–3-year-olds, and for sixteen 3–4-year-olds.

Some differences between nurseries and playgroups have already been discussed such as regards opening hours and children's age. Other differences concern activity plans, facilities and contacts with parents. The activities in nurseries are adapted to children who stay for the whole day. Children's care gains considerable attention (sleeping, dressing, washing, changing nappies, eating). These activities take much time. During peak times, when caregivers are busy with such activities, the children who already have had their turn, or who are waiting for a turn, enjoy themselves in free play. Since children in playgroups come for only a few hours a day and generally are older than nursery children, far less time is spent on care activities. Children come primarily to play and often educators organise special group activities with paint, paper and glue, play dough and games. Such activities are organised in nurseries as well, but due to the difference in children and in function these activities occur proportionally less.

The available facilities partly reflect a difference in activities. Nurseries have bedrooms, a kitchen and adapted bathroom facilities. Playgroups do not have bedrooms, and the kitchen and bathroom facilities are limited to a functional minimum. The housing situation for nurseries is generally better than for playgroups. The recent enormous growth in the number of nurseries could be realised only by building new centres. These centres were purpose-built as nurseries, whereas many playgroups have a few rooms in a community centre or in an old primary school. Through decoration and furniture these rooms have been adapted to their function and to small children. However, it is often clear that these rooms were not intended for young children, as special safety measures with steps, position of windows, water hoses and bathrooms and the lack of a special place for wet activities reveal.

Many children in a nursery have two working parents, double income parents, or a single parent who is working. When parents bring their children, they have little time to stay. This is different for parents, especially mothers, who send their children to a playgroup. The opening hours of a playgroup are too few to allow most mothers to have a job. Many have no pressing obligations while their child is in the playgroup. Therefore, such parents have more time to stay on when bringing their child or fetching them home. In effect, this means more informal parent contacts occur in playgroups than in nurseries.

It is difficult to say exactly how many playgroups and nurseries there are currently in Holland. The CBS ('Central Bureau for Statistics') counted 3766 playgroups and 1399 nurseries in 1992 (CBS, 1993).[2]

Given that the total number of child-care centres is rapidly increasing, the quality of their care and education has become a major concern. There are still few standards by which the quality of a centre can be measured. The rules drafted by the VNG state certain requirements concerning safety, hygiene, insurance, group size, opening hours, number of square meters per child, and the minimum qualification of the staff. With regard to the pedagogical quality, no minimal requirement is defined. VNG, however, suggests, that centres should guarantee the participation of parents in the formation of a centre's policy (VNG, 1991: 14).

Attempts are currently being made by centre staff and policy makers working in the field of child care to define quality standards (Hopman, 1990; Mostert, 1992). Recently, the NIZW (the Netherlands Institute of Care and Welfare) initiated a working group with the same mission (Pot, 1991) and in 1993 the Minister of Welfare, Health and Culture inaugurated a committee to advice her on the quality of child care. This committee formulated several recommendations. One recommendation concerns parents' role in the centre's education function. The committee recommended an improvement in parent–staff collaboration to ensure that child education is a joint responsibility enabled by a real partnership between parents and centre staff (Commissie Kwaliteit Kinderopvang, 1994).

Training

To become a caregiver in a child-care centre, students have to complete attendance at a senior secondary vocational school or take a course at a comparable level in the apprenticeship system. School courses take two or three years, and the course through the apprenticeship system takes two years. All courses have substantial practice periods amounting to more than 35% of all training time.

The curricula of all courses are either being developed or changed constantly due to rapid changes in the practice and policy of early childhood education. One of the important recent changes concerns the notion that workers no longer can be seen as caregivers. They are co-educators of young children (Van den Ende, 1993).

The senior secondary vocational schools offer a broad curriculum, leading to a certificate that allows students to work in a variety of professions in the health and welfare sector. The school courses vary widely in their attention to multicultural education. This variation is school and teacher dependent. Professionalisation of child care has mainly to be realised through in-service training. The apprenticeship system offers a more specialised course. The course contains eleven modules: 1) child development, 2) physical care, 3) observation and record keeping, 4) individualised help and help in groups, 5) the maintenance of classroom and play materials, 6) activities for individual children and for groups, 7) contacts with parents, 8) multicultural education, 9) prevention and remediation of problems, 10) the centre organisation and 11) working as a team. Apart from special attention for multicultural education in one of the modules, the aim of all modules is to address ways of thinking about, and handling, cultural differences. With regard to attention for multicultural education, the goal is that students acquire knowledge about different values related to multicultural situations in a centre. Students should develop an attitude of respect for differences between people, they should have an open mind towards cultural diversity and take this diversity into account when they communicate with children and parents (cf. Van den Ende, 1993). We have no precise information on how and whether the courses succeed in realising these goals.

Although no systematic comparative study has been conducted it seems that the apprenticeship students get a more effective preparation for working in child-care centres than other students. The committee on the quality of child care formed by the Minister for Welfare, Health and Culture also stated that the senior secondary vocational learning track is too broad and does not lead to an effective preparation of future child-care workers (Commissie Kwaliteit Kinderopvang, 1994).

When the apprenticeship course was started it recruited many immigrant students. Recently however, the number of immigrant students has dropped considerably. The reasons for this are: (1) the knowledge and skill requirements are relatively high and beyond the current achievement levels of many immigrant students' ability, (2) students' personal circumstances and cultural orientation hamper their possibilities to cope with the study load (POLKA, 1989).

Multicultural Education

The focus on immigrant children in Dutch institutional child care is a fairly recent phenomenon. Although immigration to the Netherlands started in the early 1960s, the Dutch journal for institutional child care 'De Kleine Wereld' (now 'Kinderopvang'), paid almost no attention between 1960 and 1975 to immigrant children or to a 'multicultural' society. In 1980, the Dutch government launched a variety of experiments. One of these experiments was the start of 12 'international nurseries'. The aim was to provide child care for immigrant children.[3] These international nurseries employed educators from immigrant groups on their staff, employed extra staff, with low costs for parents. The opening hours were adapted to parents' needs and wishes.

Since 1980, there has been a growing interest in immigrant children and multicultural education in the field of institutional child care. To illustrate some of the issues involved, we will take a look at four recent large-scale projects. Two of these projects were conducted by the VSP ('Four-City-Project'). This is an organisation in which the four largest cities in Holland work together to attempt to prevent educational disadvantage. The POLKA-project developed materials for caregiver training centres. These materials focus on better opportunities for immigrant women to complete their training as professional caregivers and to find a job in a child-care centre. The project argues that immigrant educators are important for making child-care centres more attractive to immigrant children, and for stimulating ethnic minority children's acquisition and use of their first language (VSP-W, 1992a). The KEM-project focuses on the development of methods and materials for stimulating ethnic minority children's language acquisition. By paying attention to the first and second language of these children, the project hopes to prevent learning problems (VSP-W, 1992b). The third project 'Intercultural education', planned and implemented by the NIZW ('Dutch Organisation for Care and Welfare'), is part of a larger project to support the recent expansion of nurseries. The project aims at encouraging the use of a multicultural approach with all children. It stimulates the participation of immigrant children, and extends the use of adapted methods and materials in child-care centres. Study materials have been developed to enhance caregivers' knowledge of this subject (Van Keulen & Kleerekoper, 1992). The fourth project, 'Samenspel' (Stichting 'De Meeuw') encourages immigrant parents to send their children to play-groups. The project accomplishes this by organising special afternoons in centres for immigrant mothers and their children. Mothers and children can play together and get used to the way playgroups function. After some sessions, mothers are invited to send their children to a regular playgroup (Köksal & Van der Wal, 1990; Van der Wal & Copier, 1993).

The four projects focus on different aspects, but they highlight the different activities frequently associated with multicultural education for

0–4-year-old children: the initiation of multicultural groups, the employment of immigrant staff, attempts to adapt materials and working methods,
and attempts to involve immigrant parents. In these projects, both
traditions mentioned in the section on the history of Dutch child-care
institutions are represented. Specific attention for children at risk, for
instance, is apparent in the KEM-project (a particularistic approach). The
NIZW-project focuses on quality care and education for all children,
acknowledging that this involves preparing all children for a future in the
Dutch multicultural society (a general approach).

Recently, Veen & Vermeulen (1993) completed a study on multilingual
approaches in child-care centres in the Netherlands and abroad. With
respect to the Dutch part of the study, one of their findings is that centre
staff tends to ignore attainment targets for children's language development. This implies that staff are diffident to promoting children's language
learning as a strategy to prevent later language and learning problems. The
study shows that centre staff's conception of a multilingual approach
primarily entails the use of children's first language in the centre. The use
of children's mother tongue has mainly a social and emotional function:
children should feel safe and secure, which in turn is seen as a prerequisite
for healthy and rich cognitive and language development. The study
doesn't yield information on the number of centres using a multilingual
approach.

Conclusion

The history of Dutch institutional child care is clearly shaped by the two
approaches or functions referred to in Chapter 1. The first tradition, the
particularistic one, has the longest history: the concern for the well-being
of disadvantaged children. The second tradition is general and fairly recent:
providing care and education for all children.

The present state of Dutch institutional child care shows a dynamic and
flexible situation. A centre's functioning is neither guided nor hampered
by state regulations, and the extent of parents' involvement and responsibilities are still open to discussion. The lack of regulations, however, along
with an insecure knowledge base among many professionals raises
questions on how to provide good care and education for all 0–4-year-old
children.

The quality of ECCE has become a concern for centre staff and policy
makers alike. Special attention for multicultural education in ECCE,
however, is of a recent date and the impact on training, for example, is very
limited.

We have clarified that developments in ECCE in general have affected multicultural education. The distinction of a general and particularistic approach important for the development of ECCE also influences the development of multicultural education in ECCE.

Notes

1. In 1985, the kindergartens were integrated with primary schools. The primary school is now compulsory for all five-year-old children, but almost all four-year-olds also attend the new primary school.
2. Only centres registered by the Chamber of Commerce were included in the statistics.
3. It was acknowledged that ethnic minority parents had a need for child care. The solutions available to them (sending their child to their homeland, to a Dutch substitute parent, keeping older children from school to let them take care of the children) were seen as inadequate.

3 Multicultural Education in Dutch Nurseries and Playgroups

We used two methods to obtain a picture of multicultural education in child-care centres in the Netherlands:

(1) A telephone survey (80 centres)

(2) Visits to 10 centres

To assemble a picture of current practice in multicultural education for the under fives, we carried out a telephone survey with 80 Dutch child-care centres (nurseries and playgroups) working with a multicultural approach. The centres were selected by regional child-care support centres. We asked all these regional centres to provide us with addresses of child-care centres which they deemed were active with multicultural education. We gave them no further specification and put no limit to the number of centres they could mention. We received a list of 137 centres. Most were located in the densely populated western provinces and few in rural areas. We selected all the centres in rural areas and made a random selection of centres from the remaining list until we had 80 centres. The sample is not representative of all nurseries and playgroups in the Netherlands. The selected centres all worked with ethnic minority children. No centre used a multicultural approach with a Dutch homogeneous group of children, although we assume that such centres do exist in Holland.

From the sample of 80 centres, we selected 10 centres for visits. We chose centres that represented a broad variety of approaches. The visits aimed at increasing and deepening our knowledge of the content of multicultural education in practice. Through the visits, we also obtained a picture of practical solutions to dilemmas inherent to multicultural education. During these visits we observed the daily practices and had lengthy interviews with members of staff.

The Telephone Survey

We always asked to speak with the highest ranking staff member with a supervising or managerial function. The interviews with such staff aimed to provide information about:

- the centre's context (type of centre, location, number of ethnic minority children attending the centre, number of ethnic minority caregivers);
- the centre's history (year in which the ethnic minority children started to attend the centre, persons initiating the multicultural approach, the preeminent multicultural activity;)
- parent contacts (number of home visits, differences between Dutch parents and ethnic minority parents in contacts at the beginning or end of the day, their participation in parent meetings, their participation on the board or in a parents' committee);
- views on multicultural education (specific activities seen as part of multicultural education).

The context of the centres

Thirty-three of the participating centres were playgroups and 28 nurseries. The remaining 19 centres had a combined playgroup and nursery provision, or they provided special facilities or were, preparatory kindergarten classes for three-year old children connected with a primary school, or provided child minding facilities in centres for adult education.

Forty-seven of the 80 centres interviewed are located in the western provinces of The Netherlands. Of these, 21 centres are found in the four largest Dutch cities Amsterdam, Rotterdam, The Hague, and Utrecht, where most immigrant families live (see Chapter 1).

In most of the centres (56%), the population of immigrant children is 30% or less. We found no clear correlation between the type of centre and the proportion of ethnic minority children attending the centre.

Sixty-eight per cent of the centres employed educators with an ethnic minority background. In ten centres, the number of immigrant caregivers exceeds that of native Dutch caregivers. The presence of immigrant caregivers is clearly related to the percentage of immigrant children attending the centres. The percentage of immigrant educators on the staff increases proportionately with a rising percentage of ethnic minority children in the centre (Pearson product moment correlation = 0.62; $p <$ 0.001).

The history of the centres

Figure 3.1 shows that in about half of the centres (41 out of 80) the experience with immigrant children began in the 1980s. In 24 centres, this has only happened in the last few years. This means that 30% of the centres have less than three years' experience with ethnic minority children, being partly due to the inauguration of some of the centres.

In most centres, the staff were responsible for initiating a multicultural approach. Other frequently mentioned initiators were coordinating bodies, local authorities and staff of the Educational Priority Areas Programme (OVB).[1] From their answers, it is clear that many centres did not distinguish starting to work with multicultural education from starting to work with immigrant children. Fifty per cent of the centres (40 centres) mentioned recruiting immigrant children or starting a centre intended for immigrant children as their first multicultural activity. Seventeen centres began multicultural education by nurturing staff's expertise through in-service training or the appointment of immigrant caregivers. Nineteen centres had begun by paying attention to cultural habits or rituals as regards food and special festivities, or by buying play material or books reflecting different cultures in society. For eight centres, it was impossible to name a specific activity. In such centres, multicultural education was something that had gradually evolved and developed.

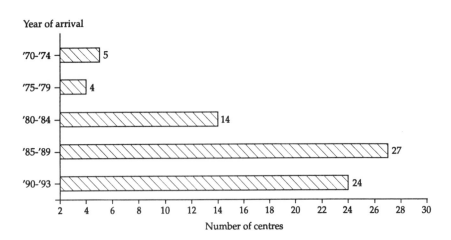

Figure 3.1 Ethnic minority children's year of arrival in the centres

We also asked for a short description of what had changed since the beginning of a multicultural approach. The most frequently mentioned changes concerned: communication with parents (29% of the centres), adaptation of decorations and play material (35%), a priority policy for migrant children, mainly referring to a special recruitment strategy (11%), adaptations of the pedagogical approach (16%), and staff's attitudes towards migrant children and parents (39%).

Parent contacts

We asked the centres about the frequency of their home visits. We were interested in home visits since home–centre contacts are seen as important in facilitating children's transition between home and centre. We were somewhat disappointed by the answers. Staff of 69 centres (86%) makes no home visits and seven (9%) visit once a year.

Parent contacts are possible via informal contacts when parents bring or pick up the children, and also in parent meetings. About 60% of the centres claim there is no difference in informal contacts between Dutch and immigrant parents. Only 17 centres say that the informal contacts with immigrant parents are less frequent and less intensive. The biggest difference between Dutch and immigrant parents appears during parent meetings. All centres organise these meetings, and forty centres (50%) experience less participation from immigrant parents during such parent meetings.

We were also interested in the reported participation of immigrant parents on the centre's board or in a parents' committee. Evidently, ten centres had no board or parents' committee. Twenty-three centres (29%) had a board, but without parents participating on this board. Forty-three centres (54%) had a board or parents' committee in which parents participated, but in only four (5%) did immigrant parents participate.

Views on multicultural education

We asked the interviewees to evaluate statements characterising multicultural education. Table 3.1 lists the different characteristics and the number of centres that did and did not deem these characteristics part of multicultural education. Not all the interviewees could or would evaluate all statements. This is also shown in the table.

The table shows that every listed characteristic is seen as an important part of multicultural education by the majority of the centres. There is, however, some variation. 'The encouragement of a positive attitude

Table 3.1 Different characteristics of MCE and centres' evaluation as to whether these are important or not

	Yes	No	?
Give children knowledge about different cultures	64 (80%)	7 (9%)	9 (11%)
Encourage a positive attitude towards representatives of other cultures by teaching them values and standards reflecting respect and acceptance	74 (93%)	4 (5%)	2 (3%)
Change in teachers' attitude and behaviour towards other cultures	66 (83%)	11 (14%)	3 (4%)
Pay due attention to differences in food and sleeping habits and hygiene	62 (78%)	3 (4%)	15 (18%)
Adapt the room and materials	58 (73%)	15 (19%)	7 (9%)
Stimulate children's development	52 (65%)	9 (11%)	19 (24%)
Prevent educational problems	61 (76%)	7 (9%)	12 (15%)
Encourage the use and stimulate the development of minority children's first language	46 (58%)	31 (39%)	3 (4%)
Support parents in their education and care	46 (58%)	7 (9%)	27 (34%)
The presence of ethnic minority children	63 (79%)	14 (18%)	3 (4%)
The presence of Dutch children	62 (78%)	11 (14%)	7 (9%)
The presence of ethnic minority teachers	68 (85%)	12 (15%)	0 (0%)
An active policy to attract ethnic minority children	60 (75%)	15 (19%)	5 (6%)
An active policy to attract ethnic minority teachers	71 (89%)	7 (9%)	2 (3%)

towards representatives of other cultures by teaching values and standards reflecting respect and acceptance' is seen by almost all the centres (74) as being very important in multicultural education. The presence and employment of ethnic minority caregivers is also seen as important in a multicultural approach.

'The encouragement of the use and stimulating the development of minority children's first language' is evaluated by almost 40% of the centres as of little importance to multicultural education. The 'no' answers were mostly given by centres with less than 20% immigrant caregivers. There is some logic in this, because without immigrant caregivers, it is difficult to pay due attention to immigrant children's first language. It is interesting to note the ambivalence about the characteristic 'support parents in their education and care'. Almost 35% of the centres were not sure if this should be seen as part of multicultural education. A similar pattern is found with regard to 'stimulate children's development' and 'prevent educational problems'. Perhaps centre staff conceive of these characteristics as more general quality characteristics than as something that is specific to multicultural education, or they are simply seen as falling beyond the centre's responsibility.

The Visits

To gain more in-depth knowledge of multicultural education in Dutch centre-based child care, we paid a visit to 10 centres. These were selected from the 80 centres participating in the survey. The main selection criterion was diversity as regards multicultural approaches. By looking at a variety of centres, we wanted to gain more understanding of the different multicultural approaches and of the factors influencing these approaches.

During the visits, information was collected through:

- a questionnaire, focusing on background data;
- interviews with the headmistress (or coordinator/director) and with one of the caregivers, focusing on basic assumptions regarding child care and multicultural education, on the curriculum and their approach to children and parents;
- observation of the activities, play material and decoration in one or two groups.

In this section, we will present the results focusing on the general characteristics of the centres, group and staff composition, parent contacts, working methods, and views on multicultural education.

General information

The centres we visited were drawn from the length and breadth of the Netherlands. Six centres are located in the four biggest cities in the Netherlands (Amsterdam, Rotterdam, The Hague and Utrecht). The other four are sited in smaller cities in the southern, central and eastern part of the Netherlands.

Centre A is a nursery in Amsterdam. It is located in an area in which 60% of the families come from ethnic minority groups (Turkish, Moroccan, Surinamese, and Antillian). The centre started about ten years ago after the neighbourhood expressed its need for child-care facilities. The centre has two infant groups, each with eight 0 to 1 year old children, and four toddler (1–4 years) groups, each with 12 children. Each group has two caregivers.

Centre B is also in Amsterdam. This is a playgroup that is part of a community centre. Some 45% of the families in the neighbourhood belong to an ethnic minority group. The centre started ten years ago in response to the need of people living in the area. The centre has three morning groups with fourteen 2- to 4-year-old children, and three afternoon groups, each for about six 1- to 2-year-olds. Each group has one caregiver and one trainee or a parent to assist.

Centre C is a nursery in Amsterdam that started 13 years ago as part of an organisation in support of Surinamese immigrants. At first, only Surinamese children attended the centre, but after a few years the board decided also to enrol 'white' children. The children come from different parts of Amsterdam. The centre has one infant and one toddler group each with about 14 children. The infant group has one caregiver and the toddler group has two caregivers. A trainee assists in one of the groups.

In Rotterdam, we visited Centre D, a fairly new nursery. It started in 1991 as the result of national and local policy to increase the number of nurseries. The centre lies in the southern part of Rotterdam in an area that is populated by a large percentage of immigrant families. Their backgrounds are diverse, but mainly Surinamese, Antillian, and Cape Verdian. The centre has two infant groups with nine children and two caregivers each. The three toddler groups each have about eight children and one caregiver. The centre has several trainees who may assist in the groups.

In The Hague, we visited a fifteen year old nursery (Centre E). It originally started as a playgroup in response to parents' demand. From 1984 to 1986, this nursery participated in the government experiment 'International Nurseries' (see Chapter 2). The nursery is situated in an area with a large percentage of ethnic minority families and a high unemployment rate. The area has a bad name because of crime and racial tensions. The nursery works with three age groups: groups for children 0 to 1 (one group), 1 to 2 (one group), and 2 to 4 (three groups). Every group contains about twelve children. The youngest age group has three caregivers. The other groups each have two caregivers.

Centre F is a playgroup in Utrecht, a city in the middle of Holland. This playgroup is part of a community centre. It started ten years ago as an activity deemed appropriate for a community centre in response to a growing demand. In the last decade, the area in which the centre is situated has experienced a large influx of immigrant families, mostly Turkish and Moroccan. In 1988, the community centre decided to actively recruit ethnic minority children until the composition of the groups reflected that of the neighbourhood. To achieve this, the centre inaugurated additional groups in the afternoon. They now have four groups for 2- to 4-year-olds. Each group has about 12 children and is led by one caregiver and one trainee.

The next centre (G) is a playgroup in Den Bosch, the capital city of a southern Dutch province. The initiative to start this playgroup was taken by an elementary school that received a growing number of immigrant children with developmental problems, such problems being evident when first entering the schools. Some 20% of the people living in the area have an ethnic background other than Dutch. These families are concentrated in a specific part of the area, commonly called 'little Turkey'. The playgroup is part of a community centre. It has one group with nine children (aged 2–4) and one caregiver.

In Leerdam, a small city near Utrecht, we visited a Turkish playgroup (Centre H). Like Centre G, this playgroup was set up after primary schools noticed developmental problems in ethnic minority children starting school. In cooperation with the local authority, a large scale educational plan with three phases was developed. The last two phases are meant for schoolchildren and the first phase is for preschool children. The start of a playgroup for Turkish children in 1991 was part of this first phase. The children begin with a home-based intervention programme, and when they reach the age of 3 they can enter the playgroup.

In Gorkum we visited Centre I, another playgroup. This playgroup started some 25 years ago as a private initiative, through the charity of some prominent citizens in Gorkum. It is housed in an old kindergarten building surrounded by old tenement buildings in which many Surinamese, Turkish and Moluccan families live. In the past the centre mainly offered children a place to play. Currently, it also aims to create learning opportunities for children from a low socio-economic background. The centre has one group a day with 16 children aged 2–4 and two caregivers.

For the last centre (J), we travelled to a nursery in the eastern part of Holland, namely Apeldoorn. Originally, the centre operated as a play-group, but two years ago they changed into a nursery because of the demand for child care for children aged 0–4. The centre is situated in an area with almost no ethnic minority families. There is one infant group (0–2) and one toddler group (2–4). The infant group has eight children and the toddler group contains thirteen children. Each group has two caregivers.

Most centres are located in neighbourhoods with a substantial proportion of immigrant families. Centre J is the only exception. The main reason for starting the centres is 'the needs of people in the neighbourhood' (Centres A, B, E, F and J). Two were started to prevent developmental problems in children (Centres G and H). One centre (I) is the result of charitable enterprise, one (D) originates from recent national and local policy measures and one (C) was started to support a particular immigrant group.

The caregiver–child ratio differs strikingly in these centres. For infant groups, the ratios vary between 1:4 (Centres A, E, and J) and 1:14 (Centre

Table 3.2 Type of centre and centre population

Centre	Type	Number of children	% imm. children	% imm. caregivers	First imm. child
A	Nursery	64	40	25	1983
B	Playgroup	60	60	0	1982
C	Nursery	22	50	100	1980
D	Nursery	51	80	75	1991
E	Nursery	72	80	60	1984
F	Playgroup	44	70	20	1987
G	Playgroup	9	70	100	1990
H	Playgroup	30	100	100	1991
I	Playgroup	35	20	0	1983
J	Nursery	35	10	25	1987

C), and for toddler groups between 1:6 (Centres A and E) and 1:15 (Centre H). Nurseries do not differ from playgroups in the calculation of these ratios. For our analyses we did not take the assistance of trainees or parents into consideration.

All nurseries are open every weekday between 8.00 and about 17.00 or 18.00 'o clock. Playgroups also are open every weekday, but children can attend either in the morning (8.30–12.00) or in the afternoon (12.30–16.00). Centres B and F have groups in the morning and in the afternoon. Centres G and I have morning-only groups and I has an afternoon-only group.

Table 3.2 provides information about the type of centre (nursery or playgroup), the number of children attending the centre, the percentage of immigrant children (rounded to whole numbers) and of immigrant caregivers, plus the year the first immigrant child entered the centre.

It is interesting to note that as compared to schools in the Netherlands child-care centres. are relatively small in size. An ideology of efficiency, which argues that small schools are not cost effective and should merge, is still rare or absent in national and local policy on child-care centres.

All centres have immigrant children and most have immigrant caregivers. Differences between centres, however, are considerable. The last column shows that centres also differ considerably in their years of experience in dealing with immigrant children. The table clearly shows that differences as regards the mentioned characteristics of centres of the same type appear to be larger than differences between nurseries and playgroups.

All the centres cover their costs with payments from the parents and the local authority. With the exception of Centre C, all nurseries have also sold child-care places to companies. Staff in Centre A expressed the fear that, in the near future, they would have to sell more places to companies and that this would mean fewer immigrant children would get a place. All centres except J, work mainly with children from low income families. Upper and middle class, white Dutch children are mainly present in the four nurseries with company-sponsored places. This underlines the fear expressed by staff in Centre A, that if centres have to sell more places to companies, fewer immigrant children, who come mainly from low income families, will find a place in a nursery.

The differences we pointed out thus far reflect a lack of national rules for the organisation and quality of child-care centres. Most centres are part of a larger child-care organisation. These organisations have a board that defines centre policy.

The group and staff composition of the centres

In the description of general features, of the centres we indicated for each centre whether it is situated in a neighbourhood with immigrant families. In Table 3.3 we present information on centres' policies for the recruitment of children and staff and whether a special policy for recruiting immigrant children results in a representation of immigrant children in the centres that is proportional to the number of immigrant families in the neighbourhood.

Table 3.3 Recruitment policies and ethnic composition of groups and staff

Centre	Recruitment policy imm. children	Recruitment policy imm. staff	% imm. children : % imm. families	% imm. children : % imm. staff
A	No	No	Lower	Higher
B	No	Yes	Higher	Higher
C	Yes	Yes	Higher	Lower
D	No	No	Balanced	Balanced
E	No	No	Higher	Higher
F	Yes	Yes	Higher	Higher
G	No	No	Higher	Lower
H	Yes	Yes	Higher	Balanced
I	No	No	Lower	Higher
J	No	No	Balanced	Higher

We also inquired whether the proportion of ethnic minority staff matched the proportion ethnic minority children.

The information in the table is insufficient for wholly answering the question as to whether special recruitment policies for immigrant children do contribute to achieving the goal of immigrant children in the centre reflecting the proportion of immigrant families in the neighbourhood. Centres with a special policy all have a higher proportion of immigrant children than the proportion immigrant families in the neighbourhood. However, there are also centres without a policy that also have a higher proportion. These are Centres B and G. Centre G uses specific eligibility criterion. The centre is meant for children, either white Dutch or immigrant children, who lack fluency in speaking the Dutch language. Proportionally more immigrant than white Dutch children meet this criterion. The criterion is defined in such a way that the centre almost has a recruitment strategy for immigrant children. Thus in Centre G, after all a special recruitment strategy may be effective. A special recruitment policy favouring immigrant children, may lead to more immigrant children entering the centre. Another direct and indirect effect of a special recruitment policy may be 'white flight'. This happened in Centre F. They recruited more immigrant children, but consequently some white Dutch parents decided to send their children to another centre. The coordinator stated 'For some people in the neighbourhood, we have become a "black" playgroup. That is why they decide to look for a playgroup with a more "white" appearance'.

Although almost all centres agree that it is important to have a representative proportion of immigrant children, this is not the reason why Centres C, F, and H have a special recruitment policy. Centres C and H focus on specific immigrant groups, Surinamese and Turkish respectively. Centre C follows a culture maintenance model and Centre H has a language policy in which mother tongue tuition is important. Centre F also stimulates immigrant children's first language use. They have special groups for Moroccan and Turkish children. The centre staff belief in the value of their care approach and need a special recruitment strategy to guarantee the further development and use of this approach. Centres without a special recruitment policy for immigrant children have various reasons for such absence. A director of Centre A pointed out that there is an enormous shortage of places. The centre has a waiting list of 200 children. In this situation, the centre is of the opinion that a special recruitment strategy is not a realistic option. Other centres did not deem such a strategy important since they already have a representative proportion of immigrant children or even an over representation (Centres D and E).

Special recruitment policies for immigrant staff seem less effective in achieving the goal of balancing the proportion of immigrant children and immigrant staff. A director of the centre in The Hague gave a possible reason: 'Given the shortage of qualified caregivers in this region, we are glad to find a caregiver, be it an immigrant or not'. Only Centre C has an immigrant director. The directors of the nine remaining centres all are Dutch.

Centres B and I employ Dutch-only caregivers. The other eight centres were asked if immigrant caregivers were assigned additional roles besides their general role as an educator. In Centres C, D and E, this was not so. In the other centres, these caregivers had additional roles. With regard to immigrant mothers and children, the caregivers worked as interpreters (Centres G and H) and as contact facilitators (Centres F, G and H). Centre A mentioned contact facilitation with regard to Dutch parents and children. In Centres F and H, immigrant caregivers have an essential role in stimulating the use of the children's home language. The Turkish educator in Centre H also played an active part in recruiting Turkish children for the playgroup. She visited the parents to explain the importance of a playgroup, and that it was not meant to function as a kind of Islamic school. She already knew a lot of mothers because she had worked with them on a home intervention programme.

With regard to the staff, the immigrant caregivers were seen as an information source as regards other cultures (Centre A). Centre A, moreover, was the only centre with special facilities for immigrant caregivers. Once a month, one morning they were free from other duties to speak to each other about their cultures, the way they themselves were educated, and how this might affect their activities and relationships in the centre.

Parental contact

In all the centres, parent contacts are seen as important. Often parent contact is necessary to establish a relationship based on mutual trust. 'If parents feel at home in the centre, so will their children'. Centres E and G believe good parent contact is also a help in exchanging information about children and their (cultural) background. When asked what the centre had to offer parents, the answers were twofold: support and relief in the education and care of the children, and to function as a place were parents could meet other parents.

Centres differ in the way they organise parent contacts. Table 3.4 gives an overview of the informal and formal contacts, home visits, parents'

Table 3.4 Informal and formal parent contacts in nurseries and playgroups

Centre	Inform contacts	Org. meetings	Educ. meetings	Parent conv.	Home visits	Parents assist.	Parents' comm.
Nurseries							
A	Many	+	+	+	+	-	+
C	Few	+	-	+	+	-	+
D	Few	+	+	-	-	-	-
E	Few	+	+	+	-	-	+
J	Many	+	+	+	-	-	+
Playgroups							
B	Many	-	-	-	+	+	-
F	Many	-	-	-	+	-	-
G	Many	-	+	+	-	+	-
H	Few	+	+	-	-	+	-
I	Few	+	+	-	+	-	+

assistance of caregivers and parent committees. Informal contacts are contacts between parents and caregivers when parents bring their children to the centre or take them home. Formal contacts are either meetings for all parents to inform them about organisational matters (henceforth termed organisational meetings), meetings to give parents educational information or to discuss educational matters (henceforth called educational meetings), or meetings between a caregiver and a parent to discuss individual children's behaviour and developmental progress (henceforth termed parent conversations). All centres organise discussions with parents before initial entry to a centre. Centre B does this during a home visit while the other centres have intake conversations taking place in the centre.

Informal contacts are an important instrument in facilitating contact between parents and staff. Often these contacts are not organised, although in most centres parents are given the opportunity to sit down and chat over a drink of coffee or tea. In Centres B and F, these contacts are part of the daily routine. In Centre F, staff are given extra time to spend on informal contact with parents. In centres with few informal contacts, staff suggested that parents have little time to pause in the morning because of their other commitments. Nursery parents go to work, as may some playgroup parents. In Centre H, the centre for Turkish children, many parents attend parent activities while their children are in the playgroup. They discuss educational topics, obtain information on health issues and follow Dutch language classes. Another reason for a low frequency and intensity of informal contacts was mentioned by staff, namely, immigrant parents' attitude embedded in the statement — 'they drop their children'.

Both nurseries and playgroups organise formal meetings. Only one playgroup (G) has parent meetings to discuss individual children's behaviour and development. Centre A is the only centre organising separate educational meetings for immigrant parents. In the other centres immigrant parents participate less frequently and less intensively in formal meetings than 'white' Dutch parents.

Four centres organise home visits. Centre B organises home visits for children now to the centre. The other three centres have them on rare occasions, for instance, only when a child shows prolonged problematic behaviour. It is a pity that home visits are so rare, since, as stated earlier, this is probably the best way for a caregiver to get to know a child's home situation, and help caregivers ease each child's transition between home and the centre.

Nurseries do not ask parents to assist staff while three playgroups have such cooperation. They perceive this as a means to inform parents on how the centre works and to teach them about child care and education. At the same time, it is clear that parental help compensates for insufficient caregivers. Centre I invites parents to assist during the first few weeks a child attends the centre. Mothers learn about the centre, and for the child, the transition between home and centre is facilitated.

We were also interested in the way parents influence the centre's functioning. Different ways by which parents could express their wishes were mentioned. Five centres had a parents' committee. Four nurseries have such a committee, as did only one of the playgroups. These committees advise and support staff, although decision making remains with the staff. This is a clear limitation on the committee's influence. In Centre E, some power is given to the parents' committee in that they have to approve of the centre's policy plan. Centre J mentioned the influence of the parents' committee in changing the group sizes in the centre. Very few immigrant parents participated in a parents' committee.

Since parents' chance to influence the centre's organisation through a parents' committee is limited, it is important for parents to have others ways to let their voice be heard. Parents generally have ample opportunity to express their wishes in less formal settings (e.g. through informal contacts). Sometimes, staff explicitly ask parents whether they have particular wishes or needs, but most of the time, parents themselves have to take the initiative. Recently, Centre C placed a suggestion box in the centre inviting parents to express their needs, wishes and complaints. The caregivers in this centre believe that, compared to Dutch parents, Surinamese parents express fewer wishes because of their great confidence in professional educators in general. Centre E also puts an extra effort in finding out about parents wishes. In 1989 they conducted a survey among all parents as a step towards the improvement of the quality of work in the centre, and to accord more with parents' wishes. In this centre, as in other centres, not all parental wishes can be fulfilled. Often requests are only taken into consideration if the proposed change would benefit all the children (Centres A, C and I). Wishes concerning hygiene, food, or clothing of the children may sometimes lead to changes, but those regarding group size or opening hours are often not open to negotiation.

Dutch parents compared with immigrant parents are seen as taking more initiative in seeking contact with the staff and in expressing their wishes. The reasons given for this difference vary. Centres E, G and I attribute this to the language barrier among immigrant parents, and Centres B and C to immigrant parents' attitude or expectation that a caregiver knows best. In Centre H, the Turkish parents are thought to express few wishes because they are not familiar with centre-based child care. To stimulate the involvement of all parents, Centre G developed a formal policy. Each primary caregiver signs a contract stating that she will assist staff at least four days a year, that she will assist with festivities and trips, that she attends educational meetings and permits caregivers to make home visits. If mothers do not comply, their children could lose their place in the centre.

Conflicts between centre staff and parents also are informative as to parents' wishes. A few conflicts with parents were mentioned during the interviews. In Centre C some years ago, a conflict arose with the Surinamese parents in the parents' committee. The nursery wanted a free day to commemorate Surinam independence day. The parents' committee did not agree because they would be forced to take a day off from work. They argued that living in Holland required adaptation to the Dutch system. Another conflict was with a Surinamese mother who reckoned the caregivers spoke too much Sranantongo (one of the Surinamese languages) in the nursery. In Centre H, a Turkish father complained that his son's caregiver paid too much attention to Christmas. The caregiver argued that living in Holland meant adapting to certain Dutch customs. Moreover, she had suggested that a celebration of Christmas is something very common in Dutch primary schools. Children and parents need to become accustomed to such events.

Centres also mentioned conflicts between parents. In Centre F, there are sometimes tensions between Dutch and immigrant parents culminating in apparent discriminatory remarks. Caregivers decided to correct parents immediately when such incidences happen. Caregivers in Centre G have also witnessed similar conflicts between parents. Neither these two centres or any of the other centres has a formal anti-racism policy.

Working methods of the centres

First a short impression is given of the working method and social atmosphere in each of the centres.

Centre A aims to offer its children effective care in a safe and familiar environment, along with an opportunity to play in a group with other children (social development). They strive to function as complementary to education at home. The whole centre was originally designed for use as a nursery. In the centre's rooms we saw special facilities for the children, for instance a play tower which could only be used by children and not by adults. Staff stressed that a nursery should not be assigned the task of preventing disadvantages or countering major developmental problems. Nor does the nursery prepare the children for primary school in any specific way. During our observation period, no child was isolated. Stimulation of the cognitive development of children was incorporated in the daily routine: reading aloud to the children, group discussions, making an Easter bunny and naming the colours of the eggs.

The language of the centre is Dutch. Staff argued that there are too many language groups represented in the centre to actively stimulate children's home language: but they encourage parents to speak their mother tongue at home. Another argument presented was that the immigrant parents prefer the Dutch language to be developed in the nursery. The centre participates in a project on multilingualism (the KEM-project; see Chapter 2). In the group we observed, we did not find a multilingual approach in the activities and materials. We found only one non-Dutch book.

Centre B's main goal is to offer children opportunities for play with peers and to develop motor skills. On the morning we visited the centre, most of the time was spent on free play and in a gymnastics class. Apart from this, some time was spent on eating and drinking, story reading and singing.

The interviewees stated that the relative freedom children get in the centre is expected to increase children's sense of confidence and security. Caregivers use few rules for regulating social behaviour. A consequence of this approach of stressing play and freedom was that individual children received little attention. Children were rather noisy. Staff only interfered when children were aggressive, hurt other children or when they started throwing sand from the sandbox on the floor.

The staff pay special attention to immigrant children's Dutch language development. The activities include language games and a library project with book-reading sessions for immigrant children. The overall language in the centre is Dutch. This is also the wish of the parents. Parents and trainees used the children's home language to assist the children and to make them feel at home in the centre.

The staff are opposed to the idea that the centre should prepare children for primary school. They think it is more important to offer children an opportunity to have fun and play together.

Centre C aims to provide a secure environment to encourage children's development. Caregivers hope that children will acquire rules necessary for living together, for example to be polite and friendly. They were rather strict with the older children. As a caregiver stated 'It is very important that children learn what they can and cannot do'. We observed that the African Surinamese caregivers (all but one) were very strict and directive if children did something wrong, for instance slapping other children or playing with food. The centre believes the Dutch parents are sometimes too free with the children and show too much tolerance. Of all the centres we visited, this was the only one where parents, caregivers and children took their shoes off in the hallway. The language in the centre is Dutch. This is the language parents prefer.

Centre D seeks to offer children a place in which they feel happy and respected. The new building in which the centre is located makes a child-friendly impression, where children can freely interact with other children and adults.

We observed caregivers working quite intensively with the children. We were surprised, however, by the lack of activities in which the children could communicate and learn to play together, for instance via group conversation. As to rules for social behaviour, we saw a fairly relaxed and unrestrained approach. The children had to follow some rules, but there was often no punishment if they did not comply. This resulted at times in a somewhat chaotic atmosphere. The activities for the children seemed the result of spontaneous, creative ideas of the caregivers. Children's preparation for primary school is not seen as an important goal. Staff was the opinion that this preparation happens anyhow. Caregivers try to improve children's emotional wellbeing. The language of the centre is Dutch.

Centre E aims to offer a safe yet challenging environment for children, where the children can meet other children and adults. Special attention is sometimes paid to immigrant children's language development and play. Preparation for the primary school is deemed an unimportant goal. The staff argued that any centre offering good child care gives children a good primary school preparation. Unfortunately, we did not observe a variety of different activities, because the weather was beautiful and the children went outside to play. The use of the home language is seen as important for the children's self-esteem, and for their overall language competence. During our visit, the attention to home languages was signalled when everybody wished each other an enjoyable dinner in four different languages (Arab, Shranantongo, Turkish and French). We found only a few books in other languages; one was in Arabic, two were in English.

Stimulating children's development and the prevention of potential disadvantage are important goals to the staff of Centre F. Stimulation of language development is seen as very important for immigrant and for Dutch children alike. In the bilingual groups, the Turkish and Moroccan children are encouraged to use their home language. Caregivers work with the 'one person–one language' strategy. Their concern for home languages was evident in the Turkish and Moroccan books we found in the playgroup. The focus on home languages is not always applauded by the immigrant parents. These parents prefer the Dutch language to be developed in the centre. If a parent protests, staff attempts to transfer the child from the bilingual group to another group. The centre tries to prepare children for primary school. Some children attend the centre three days instead of two when they are almost four years of age — that is the age for the transfer to primary school.

In Centre G as in Centre F, the prevention of deprivation and disadvantage in children is seen as a primary aim. The focusing of this aim is mainly on children's language development and the development of motor skills. The general approach is rather academic. This is deemed particularly necessary to those children already diagnosed as having language problems. Despite the rather academic approach, language stimulation was offered in a playful manner on the day we visited the centre. The caregiver asked every child gliding on the slide questions such as 'What colour is your sweater?' If they gave the correct answer they could glide down the slide.

Although caregivers in Centre G stated that they oppose the idea of the centre preparing children for primary school, they paradoxically suggest that children should know how to behave in a group. They also use a specific language method to prepare children for working with a similar language learning method in primary schools.

The language of the playgroup is Dutch. This is the parents' wish. Parents are encouraged to speak their mother tongue with the children. Caregivers argue that it is important for mothers to be able to communicate with their children. In the centre we saw some Turkish books, and there were tapes with Turkish and Moroccan music and Koranic texts.

Staff of Centre H want their children to enjoy playing. Besides this, caregivers aim to facilitate the transition to primary school by organising developmentally enriching activities. For all children who transfer to primary school (at four years old) caregivers complete a checklist assessing children's knowledge, skills and behaviour. They discuss their assessment with the children's primary school teacher. Attempts are being made to stimulate children's cognitive development. The centre makes use of the 'KOST-programme' (a programme designed to observe and actively stimulate different aspects of children's development). During our stay at the centre, this focus on children's development was obvious. During singing periods, the children were invited to sing with a microphone before the whole group. The caregiver told us this was an effective practice to enable the children to learn to perform in public. Other activities we observed that afternoon included children playing with clay and puzzles, counting and reading aloud to the children. Time for free play was very limited. The language in the playgroup was Turkish.

Centre I aims to offer children safe and developmentally enriching play facilities. The children are given a lot of freedom in their social behaviour. During our visit the group was engaged in a language game, singing songs, painting, free play, and the caregiver twice read a story. Special attention is paid to immigrant children's (Dutch) language development.

Some time is spent on preparation for primary school. The three year old children go to a separate room to read or play with specific material. We did not observe this during our visit. The language of the centre is Dutch.

Centre J seeks to offer a safe environment in which children are able to develop naturally. The education given is not seen as extra to, but different from that given at home. It is different because it involves an interactive, group based education. During our visit the caregivers expressed a flexible but observant attitude towards the children, letting them know the rules, but also allowing them enough autonomy to feel free to speak and move and to take initiatives. Caregivers were patient, responsive and supportive while listening to children's stories.

The centre does not aim to prepare children for school. The language in the centre is Dutch.

To summarise, centres clearly differ in the type of development they want to encourage in children and in the intensity of developmental stimulation. Most centres use an open approach to children, characterised by ample opportunities for free play, freedom of choice of activities and a minimum of rules for social behaviour. Centres C and G used a more strict approach. In Centre C, more structure is given to children in order for them to learn the rules necessary for communal living. In Centre G, a structured approach is seen as necessary when working with children already diagnosed as having developmental problems. Of all centres Centre G pays most attention to preparing children for school. All centres pay special attention to children with developmental problems. We asked the centres whether they had adapted their pedagogical method to immigrant children. Half of the centres expressed that there had been no such adaptation. Centres A, B, E, F, and I offer immigrant children extra language stimulation. Centres E, F, and G pay special attention to immigrant childrens' play and motor skills.

Only one centre, Centre F, may be characterised as multilingual. This centre has monolingual Dutch groups and bilingual groups (Dutch/Turkish and Dutch/Moroccan Arabic). One centre uses mainly Dutch, but in contacts between individual caregivers and individual children they try, whenever possible, to stimulate the use of children's mother tongues. Eight centres are monolingual. Centre H is monolingually Turkish and the remaining centres are monolingually Dutch.

With the exception of Centre J, no centre had a written pedagogic plan. Five centres are still working on such a plan. Centre A and F are hesitant or reluctant because they fear that a plan would hinder their individualistic approach.

As for stimulating children's development and detecting problems, caregivers often rely on their intuition and experience. Only in Centre E do staff keep records of each child's development. Centres D and J keep some track of children's development, but not in a systematic way. Centres H and I are still in an experimental stage. Keeping track of children's development and learning progress seems especially important for centres whose mission includes preparing children for school. Centre G, however, which stresses this goal, does not keep records.

So far, the services that centres aim to offer children have been described in broad general terms. To provide more specific information, in each centre we asked one caregiver and the co-ordinator to rank the following eight goals:

G1 Provide good care (nursing) for children;
G2 Provide a safe and familiar environment for children;

G3 Prepare for primary school;
G4 Detect developmental problems in children;
G5 Stimulate children's development;
G6 Pay special attention to the prevention of deprivation in children;
G7 Transmit particular values and standards to the children;
G8 Stimulate that children play together and know each other better.

Except for Centres G and H, all the centres put G2 ('Provide a safe and familiar environment for children') in first place. This is seen as a prerequisite for all the other activities. Centres G and H both reserve the first place for G6 ('Pay special attention to the prevention of deprivation in children'). This was to be expected since these centres were originally set up to meet this goal.

On average, G3 ('Prepare for primary school') was seen as least important. One of the caregivers in Centre B put it this way: 'A playgroup should not become a school. Children have two years in Kindergarten to prepare themselves for primary school. I think it is more important that we give children the opportunity to play and have fun'. Although many activities in the centres prepare children for primary school in one way or another, the low priority of this goal is somewhat surprising, because this goal is closely linked to the main reason why immigrant parents send their child to a child-care centre, as many interviewees stated (see also Eldering & Vedder, 1992; Pels, 1991). We may take this as an indication that centres are not responsive to immigrant parents' wishes concerning the curriculum.

If we look at the average ranking the following list results:

(1) G2: Provide a safe and familiar environment for children.
(2) G8: Stimulate children to play together and know each other better.
(3) G5: Stimulate children's development.
(4) G1: Provide good care (nursing) for children.
(5) G7: Transmit particular values and standards to the children.
(6) G6: Pay special attention to the prevention of deprivation in children.
(7) G4 Detect developmental problems in children.
(8) G3 Prepare for primary school.

A difference of opinion was seen most with 'provide good care (nursing) for children' and 'pay special attention to the prevention of deprivation in children'. Some of these differences can be attributed to the type of centre: Nurseries put more emphasis on providing care and nursing, playgroups seem to focus more on the prevention of deprivation. Compare, for instance, the remark of the director of Centre E: 'Simply being at a nursery means that development is already stimulated. If your work is done right, it will not be necessary to prevent deprivation', and the following remark made by the headmistress of Centre F: 'Active stimulation of the development of children is the main goal in our playgroup and for me, this is closely linked to the prevention of deprivation'.

Views on multicultural education

We start with some impressions from each centre.

Centre A: During our observation period we did not notice any habits or activities that reminded us of other cultures. A Surinamese caregiver indicated that she practices foot massage with the children if the parents ask her to. This is an activity common in the Surinamese culture. It is supposed to encourage the muscle strength and stimulate walking activities.

The use of toys, books and other material reflecting different cultures is not a priority. The argument is that families themselves seem not interested in such material. 'They live in Holland and buy Dutch toys'. Books and music tapes were the only materials we found that reflected different cultures.

Centre B: According to the caregivers, the centre uses dolls, books and wall decorations reflecting different groups in society. In practice, however, we found almost no materials that reminded us of a multicultural society.

Centre C: During our visit the children ate bread in the morning and were served a tasty Surinamese meal of chicken and rice in the afternoon. The nursery does not have many multicultural books, toys and other materials. The staff have imported some books from Surinam.

Centre D: Caregivers in this centre are opposed to paying special attention to different cultures. During our observations, no special attention was given to the cultural background of the children. We stayed in a toddler group which contained only immigrant children and two immigrant caregivers. No books dealt with other cultures, and none of the dolls, toys, puzzles and other materials reflected a multi cultural society. The only reminders of the multicultural neighbourhood were the presence of immigrant children and caregivers and the food (Surinamese soup).

Centre E: The toys and wall displays in the nursery reflect many different cultures. We saw, for instance, cardboard dolls dressed in cloths representing different cultures, a carpet for worshipping, and posters of different countries. During our visit, all children danced to Surinamese music.

Centre F: To let the children (and parents) feel that their various cultural backgrounds are equally valued and to make them feel at home, the wall displays, toys and books in this centre reflect different cultures. We saw, for instance, a large Turkish carpet with the picture of a mosque, and a small wooden mosque in which children could play. In the groups, Dutch, Arab and Turkish songs were sung.

Centre G: In this centre, children have ample opportunities to experience differences in food, clothes, music and toys from a variety of cultures. The festivities and wall displays in the centre also reflect different cultures. On the day of our visit, the playgroup celebrated the Turkish Sugar feast with all kinds of Turkish snacks.

Centre H: It was interesting to observe how much this playgroup with Turkish staff and children resembled other playgroups in Holland. We did not see any Turkish habits for instance. Only books (but not toys, and puzzles) were adapted to the Turkish children.

Centre I: Toys and wall displays in this centre were not adapted to the presence of immigrant children. The caregivers say that this is not necessary because they care for many Dutch children from a low socio-economic background, and, according to the co-ordinator, 'there is no difference between children from a low-social-background and immigrant children'.

Centre J: The centre seeks to show the children differences and similarities between cultures. These were not empty words. Children sang a song in English and in Indonesian. One activity involved a globe on which the caregiver showed where the Turkish apprentice came from, and how to travel to Turkey. At that time, it was close to Easter, so the children were asked where on the globe the Easter bunny came from. 'Indonesia', said one of the boys.

A lot of attention is also given to multicultural wall displays, toys, and other play materials in the centre. Besides the globe, we saw an Indonesian wayang puppet, a doll's house with little white and coloured dolls, Turkish shoes and a Turkish cap, plus different posters presenting (black) children from other cultures. Books also reflected different cultures.

Almost all the centres regard multicultural education as something mainly transmitted by caregivers' attitudes. Educators should have an open mind towards different standards and values in different cultures. The centres differ, however, in their focus on 'cultural' differences. We can make a distinction between centres that resist the idea of focusing mainly on cultural differences, and centres who take cultural differences as a starting point. In the first category fall Centres B, D, E and I. These centres believe that one should focus on all children and parents as individuals, taking their diverse backgrounds into account. Multicultural education is not an exclusive approach one applies only to immigrant people. This view is most clearly represented by staff from Centre D. In their policy, there is no special focus on the presence of immigrant children, or on a special educational approach, and immigrant educators are not given any special tasks. As one of the staff said, 'We don't believe that there should be an emphasis on different cultures. Differences already get too much attention in multicultural education. We are not organising any special activities. These are often too traditional'. They consider that the term 'multicultural' is somewhat misplaced for their approach.

The other centres are more inclined to use cultural differences as a starting point, although they differ in the way they focus on immigrant children and their home culture. In J there is no special focus on these children. Their main aim is bringing Dutch children into contact with other cultures. To facilitate this, they use the presence of immigrant caregivers, toys, books, and puzzles to reflect different cultures, and recount stories about foreign people and countries. At the other pole we find Centre H. This centre focuses exclusively on Turkish children. The ample attention paid to their home culture is, for instance, reflected in the policy to speak Turkish in the centre. Centre C and G lie somewhere in-between regarding multicultural education as a way to encourage cultural exchange.

We asked the co-ordinators and caregivers to look at the following goals and rank them in order of relevance for multicultural education:

M1 Pay due attention to differences in food and sleeping habits and hygiene.
M2 Encourage a positive self image in ethnic minority children.
M3 Give children knowledge about different cultures.
M4 Encourage a positive attitude towards representatives of other cultures by teaching children values and standards reflecting respect and acceptance.
M5 Encourage co-operation and playing together by children of different cultural backgrounds.
M6 Stimulate ethnic minority children's development and prepare them for primary school.
M7 Prevent deprivation in ethnic minority children.
M8 Encourage the use and stimulate the development of minority children's first language.
M9 Encourage the use and stimulate the development of the country's majority language.

The 20 interviewees were asked to leave out aspects which they deemed not relevant for multicultural education. M6 (stimulate ethnic minority children's development and prepare for primary school), M7 (prevent deprivation in ethnic minority children), and M8 (encourage the use and stimulate the development of minority children's first language) were often not included in the ranking task. These are all particularistic aspects not relevant to many respondents. With regard to M6 and M7, interviewees argued that these were aspects important for all children, not just for immigrant children.

Almost all interviewees included M3 (give children knowledge about different cultures) and M4 (encourage a positive attitude towards representatives of other cultures by teaching children values and standards reflecting respect and acceptance). Overall these goals, which are typical of a general approach in multicultural education, were not ranked very high. The top three of ranked statements were as follows:

(1) M2: Encourage a positive self image in ethnic minority children.
(2) M7: Prevent deprivation in ethnic minority children.
(3) M5: Encourage co-operation and playing together by children of different cultural backgrounds.

The interviewees who included statement M7 in their ranking (only eight) ranked it very high. This list suggests that some staff prefer a particularistic approach rather than a general one. The survey, overall, however, showed a preference for a general approach.

The lowest ranks were given to M6 (Stimulate ethnic minority children's development and prepare them for primary school) and M1 (Pay due attention to differences in food and sleeping habits and hygiene). All but five interviewees deemed attention for differences in food and sleeping habits and hygiene an aspect of multicultural education, but they see it as a rather unimportant aspect.

Conclusion

A survey in 80 child-care centres yielded the following conclusions: There is no relationship between the type of centre (nursery or play group) and the proportion of ethnic minority children attending the centre.

The presence of ethnic minority staff is seen as an important condition or facilitator for working with a multicultural approach. A lack of ethnic minority staff is likely to mean that a centre pays little special attention to multicultural education. Another finding was that the more ethnic minority children a centre has, the more minority caregivers are present. Multicultural education is something that is closely linked to the presence of ethnic minority children. Half of the centres mentioned efforts to recruit ethnic minority children as the first multicultural priority. This clearly restricts the number of centres that implement multicultural education, although another fact is that recently, many centres have experienced an influx of ethnic minority children. This is due to an increase in the number of places available in child-care centres and to the fact that the proportion of immigrant children in the group of 0–4-year-olds is rapidly increasing. They occupy many of these new places.

We took a special interest in parent–caregiver contact. We found that almost 90% of the centres do not organise, or hardly ever organise home visits. The lack of parent–caregiver contacts at home may be compensated by daily contact when parents bring or pick up their children. From our visits, we know that the intensity and frequency of these contacts vary strongly between centres. In the survey, 20% of the centres reported that such contact with ethnic minority parents are less than the contact with 'white' Dutch parents. Furthermore, 50% of the centres reported that ethnic minority parents participate less in parent meetings. In some centres we visited, staff reported that extra efforts to increase and intensify immigrant parents' participation were successful.

Many centres have parent committees. The influence of these committees on the educational practices and organisation of the centres is very limited. Minority language parents rarely have a seat on these committees. Such committees advise and support staff, but eventually staff make strategic decisions. Wishes concerning hygiene, food or clothing of the children may sometimes lead to changes, but those regarding group size or opening hours are often not open to negotiation.

The encouragement of a positive attitude towards representatives of other cultures by teaching values and standards reflecting respect and acceptance is seen by most centres as an important goal for multicultural education. They know that, to achieve this, caregivers need to change their attitude and behaviour towards other cultures. A controversial goal concerns attention to the development of children's first language. More than half of the centres are convinced that stimulating children's first language proficiency is an important goal for multicultural education, whereas the other centres are convinced that this is not so. This same controversy was also clear from the interviews we had with the centres visited. Attention to Dutch as a second language was more generally seen as an important aspect of multicultural education. Centre staff seem to favour a general approach to multicultural education and doubt whether a particularistic approach can have a positive impact on children's development.

The main reason for starting a centre is the need of families in a neighbourhood for child care. The lack of national rules for the organisation of child-care institutions is particularly clear from the differences between centres in the caregiver–child ratio. For infants the ratio varies between 1:4 and 1:14 and for toddlers between 1:6 and 1:15. We found no relationship between centre type (nursery or playgroup) and the percentage of immigrant children and immigrant caregivers in the centre. Using a special policy for recruiting immigrant children may be effective. Special recruitment strategies for immigrant staff seem ineffective. In some regions this may be due to an overall scarcity of qualified educators. More generally, it seems that centres set high initial qualification requirements that are too high for many immigrant candidates. A recent study (Van Bennekom, Mostert & Stegenga, 1992) showed that almost 40% of all caregivers in child-care centres in one of the biggest cities and in a rural area in the Netherlands have completed training as a primary school teacher or a social worker. Rather few immigrants complete their studies at this level. There are few special courses for child-care centre staff — those that exist are relatively basic. Moreover, it seems immigrant caregivers, in practice, need more qualification than Dutch caregivers. For example, immigrant staff often have additional tasks as interpreters, bilingual assistants, home–school facilitators, and as a knowledge source on immigrant cultures.

The centres give children ample opportunities for free play. Caregivers use very few rules for social behaviour. Staff generally reject the use of structured approaches or the use of a well defined curriculum. Centres rarely monitor or record development and learning progress. Caregivers are convinced their memory is perfectly capable of capturing all the important information on each child's development. This is probably an exaggeration of caregivers capacities. Few children attend the centres for whole weeks and whole days. Therefore, a single caregiver may be responsible for more than 30 children a week. Add to this the finding that all but one centre lacked a well defined plan as to what developmental and learning goals they would want the children to achieve. The result is that caregivers may only hold a rather global notion of individual children's developmental progress.

Centre staff vary considerably as to their transmission of multicultural education. Some centres pay special attention to children's first language, whereas others stress the importance of giving children an ample opportunity to learn Dutch as a second language. The prevention of developmental and learning problems in immigrant children is also a controversial activity. A few centres give this high priority, whereas others simply neglect or reject simple attention to immigrant children, arguing that such a special focus on immigrant children will stigmatise such children. Some centres adapted wall displays and their toys and books quite extensively to signal and celebrate the presence of children from a variety of cultures. Other centres deemed this irrelevant or even undesirable.

Almost all centres suggest that goals like 'give children knowledge about different cultures' and 'teach children respect and acceptance for children from different cultural backgrounds' are important for multicultural education. The first goal is realised through activities such as celebrating festivities and eating food from different cultures. Activities are less evident to teach children to respect and accept behaviour from different cultural backgrounds.

The two most important conclusions from this chapter are: (A) Centres see multicultural education as education involving immigrant children, and (B) centres generally prefer the general function of multicultural education rather than particularistic functions.

Notes

1. OVB is a national policy dedicated to the prevention of educational disadvantage.

4 International Experiences

We studied multicultural approaches in young children's education in England, Scotland, Denmark, Sweden, Belgium, Germany, Spain and France. The goal was twofold: 1) To show the comparability of the situation in ECCE and multicultural education in ECCE institutions in a variety of European countries, and 2) clarify that the way centres operate in the different countries is influenced by particular contexts.

The institutions that we visited were specifically chosen for the varied approaches they embodied. They were either contacted because we had read about them in journals and newsletters on early childhood education, or they were introduced to us by colleagues working in the field of multicultural education. This means that they are not representative of early childhood institutions in the countries. For general descriptions of early childhood education in Western Europe countries, we refer to other studies (Mellhuish & Moss, 1991; Moss, 1988). Most of our visits took place after we had completed the visits to Dutch centres. As in the Netherlands, we used interviews and observation. A short description of each centre is provided. For such descriptions, we deemed it less appropriate to choose a format that primarily elucidates the commonalities between the centres. Instead, we try to stress each centre's uniqueness. We will focus on the situations, processes and products characterising the multicultural approaches in these European centres as distinct from that which typifies the Dutch situation.

Staff in the European centres were also asked what goals they deemed important for ECCE in general and for multicultural education in ECCE in particular. The findings will be presented and compared with the findings from the Netherlands.

England

In England, we visited a nursery class in a primary school and a nursery centre. Both were in Coventry. We had prepared for our visit by reading some studies on multicultural education in England (Fase, 1990; Troyna & Carrington, 1990; Veen & Vermeulen, 1993) and assumed that we would find abundant attention to anti-racist education and discussions about equal opportunities. It was surprising to find that the most visible and audible attention went to language education.

The nursery class was being attended by 3–4-year-old children. It is open between 9.15 and 11.45 in the morning and between 13.00 and 15.30 in the afternoon. In the morning, the class is attended by a group of 39 children and in the afternoon there is another group of 39 children. Half of the children have an English background and half are Pakistani (Panjabi). The class has three full time caregivers. Each is responsible for a group of 13 children. There is also a half time bilingual assistant (English-Panjabi) and a special needs educator. The bilingual assistant works with children to help their first and second language development and learning skills. She organises short sessions with a group of Panjabi children to stimulate either their first language development or to give English as a second language lessons. Most of the time, however, we saw her joining in the ongoing central activities. For some children, she explained a task in Panjabi or she helped to understand a message from the caregiver. Other functions of this assistant are: a) to interpret and translate during parent–caregiver inter-actions, necessary to enable parents to gain information about their child's education; b) to listen and to talk with parents in their preferred language about the education system; and c) to encourage parents to take part in school activities. The latter function concerns either parents joining the children and playing with them during one session a week, or a more formal activity for mothers such as participating in an English language course organised in the school.

The head of the nursery described the following multicultural initiatives in the nursery:

(1) The children are encouraged to talk in their mother tongue and English.
(2) There is recognition and celebration of other cultures' festivals where appropriate.
(3) All labelling (e.g. on walls) in the nursery reflects the home language of each group.
(4) Letters, notices and messages are written in each language.
(5) Multicultural books, tapes, pictures, dressing up clothes and play equipment are available.
(6) The children learn songs and rhymes in other languages.

The overall aim of these initiatives was formulated as follows: 'All children should be able to take initiatives, they should feel self assured, they should learn to respect each other and know about differences in appearances, language and cultural background'.

The nursery used a cognitive oriented curriculum. Children were engaged in book reading, and through rhymes, songs and discussions, they were stimulated to learn new concepts. This rather school-like approach was also very clear from attempts to involve parents in their children's learning. Each fortnight, the children take a worksheet home with a maths task. The idea is that the family shares the work children are doing in school and that the child, together with other family members, carries out the task. When the activity is completed the child returns the sheet to the school where it is discussed or displayed in the class. The children keep a diary of all the home activities. This diary not only informs the caregivers how successful, enjoyable and practical the activities were, but also how the family was involved. On the morning we visited the nursery, we saw the children returning the sheets when they and their parent entered the classroom. The children's enthusiasm clearly was an encouraging experience for caregivers and parents.

The most important problem for the staff regarding multicultural education was to avoid conflicts with parents about differences in preferred values. An example was an incident with a father who, in front of all children, the staff and some parents had yelled that he was fed up with the Panjabi language and the Panjabi favouring attitude of the staff. After this incident, staff had invited the father for a discussion.

The other centre, a nursery centre, tries to be a meeting point for young families and their problems. Many are single-parent families which have little support from the extended family. The families in the neighbourhood and in the centre come from a broad variety of ethnic and cultural backgrounds.

The centre works in three teams. The first team is responsible for children under 3 years. There are 35 full-time equivalent places, mostly offered on a two day programme of Monday and Thursday or Tuesday and Friday. Wednesday is a family morning session, where parents are encouraged to be closely involved. The team consists of seven professional caregivers.

The second team is responsible for children aged between 3–5 years. There are 35 full-time equivalent places, offered in a two day programme like that in the under 3 group. The number of caregivers is the same as in the first team. These two teams are supported by three bilingual language assistants.

The third team, containing five staff members, is responsible for a shared care family provision. Here parents and staff share the care of young children from 0–3 years. Toys and equipment are provided to stimulate children's play. The staff function as a model to the parents on how to care for and educate a child. Staff members are also available to support, advise or chat to adults in a relaxed atmosphere. Cookery and discussion groups are provided by the team. Behaviour management programmes can be arranged individually or in groups. Staff are also able to offer outreach work in the home. Not all parents participating in the shared care programme do so voluntary. Some parents are referred to the centre by social workers to avoid further judicial procedures and custody measures.

The centre developed an equal opportunities policy statement which reads as follows:

****

We recognise that passive policies will not in themselves provide equality of opportunity and that specific and positive attitudes and approaches are needed.

Statements of Value

- *The centre is opposed to racist and sexist attitudes and practices.*

- *We are fully committed to the active promotion of equal opportunities in our employment practices, in our work in the centre and in the provision of all our services.*

- *People are of equal worth whatever their race, culture, ability, gender, social class or religion.*

- *Though we believe all people are equal we must respect and value their differences.*

- *We are determined to make all efforts to prevent discrimination against staff, families and children regardless of their race, culture, religion, colour sex or disability.*

Statements of Intent

To ensure that the centre provides a welcoming environment to all users regardless of race, sex or disability:

- *the centre will respect and be sensitive to ethnic and cultural diversity, stereotyping and disability.*

- *racist and sexist attitudes will be challenged with staff, parents and children.*

To ensure that all children have equal access to the whole curriculum:

- *resources and displays will reflect and promote our anti-racist policy and represent gender and disability in a positive way.*

****

The staff of the centre are very much a reflection of the ethnic variety in the neighbourhood. Children speak their own language with regular staff members, and the bilingual language assistants give short lessons in English as a second language. The multiculturalism of this centre however, seems relatively more explicit in its links with the local multicultural community. The shared care provision is a clear example of this, as is the preparation with the children of a multicultural festival for the neighbourhood. In our interviews, we learned that the centre is very much involved in developing liaisons with other agencies, such as social services, health and cornerstone family centres.

Scotland

In Scotland, we visited a small centre in Edinburgh. We learned about the centre from a newsletter in which it was described as a centre actively committed to eradicating racism in all its forms, particularly institutional racism. It is actively committed to community development work leading to equality of access for members of all minority ethnic communities, with a special emphasis on equality for women. The centre was started as a meeting place and community centre for women from minority ethnic communities. Many of the women had young children. In order to have more opportunities to come to the centre and participate in all kinds of activities, they started a nursery. At first, only ethnic minority mothers' children went, but the staff found that this hampered the children's later integration into ethnically heterogeneous groups. Since then, the child centre tries to have a balance of 50% ethnic minority children and 50% white Scottish children. Most children attend the centre either in the morning or in the afternoon. The centre works with a maximum of ten children per session. On the morning we attended the group, there were one supervisor and three volunteers. Most volunteers are mothers, but some are young women who enjoy playing with children, or who saw their participation as a first step towards becoming a professional caregiver.

The supervisor was a Moroccan woman, who had taken a higher education in her country, but had no special certificate for working in a nursery. The head of the centre argued that having a representative of an ethnic minority group as a supervisor is more important to the children and their parents than having a qualified nurse. The supervisor functions as a positive role model for the children and parents, and it is easier for the parents to communicate to her than to a 'white' supervisor.

There was one other important characteristic of the centre. It had a very clear anti-racist policy. All parents, staff and groups using the centre had to comply with an anti-discrimination statement. Any complaint of a coloured person in the centre who felt discriminated against by another person in the centre or connected to the centre, was taken seriously. The experience of discrimination was taken as enough ground and had not to be proven or explained. The discriminated and discriminating person would have a discussion with the head, which is usually concluded by an apology from the discriminating person. If this person refused to apologise, he or she would lose the right to make use of, or enter the centre. So far, two incidences of discrimination had been reported and in both cases, the discriminating persons had apologised.

Denmark

In Denmark, we visited two child-care centres in Copenhagen. The first one was a government supported centre for children aged between 6 months and three years, a vuggestuen. The second was a non-subsidised centre for 0 to 6-year-old children.

With regard to multicultural education, the first centre had two interesting organisation principles. At first, this centre received children through a recruitment centre. The centre had no recruitment procedure of its own. As a consequence, the ethnic minority children in the centre (20%) represented a variety of ethnic minority groups. The staff felt that they could not satisfy the educational needs of the children from such different cultural backgrounds. They urged the recruitment centre to send them only Danish, Turkish and Moroccan children. At first, the recruitment centre would not cooperate, but after a few years, they agreed. Currently, the centre runs four groups of about ten children each. Two groups have only Danish children, one group has Danish and Turkish children and one has Danish and Moroccan children. Each group has three to four nurses. In the Turkish group, one of these nurses is Turkish and in the Moroccan group, one is a Moroccan. They play a special role in the stimulation of children's first language development and in maintaining good contacts with the Turkish and Moroccan parents. The centre is open on working days between 6.00 and 17.30.

The centre organises relatively few meetings with parents, and the staff only occasionally make home visits. To have good contact with parents, to exchange information about the children, and to ascertain parents' educational wishes and preferred strategies, the centre asks the parent who brings the child or takes him or her home, to stay every day for a short conversation with one of the nurses. This is more or less a rule of the centre to which all parents comply. Through this rule, not only parents and staff speak to each other, but parents also meet and exchange information. Parents come to know each other and their different cultural backgrounds.

An interesting characteristic of the second centre is that it didn't start as a child centre. It is a centre where ethnic minority adults, mainly women, can learn Danish. Many of these women brought their young children along. Other women, although interested in following a language course, stayed home to look after the children.

The centre was thus started as a support for parents who wanted to follow a course. It is open on working days from 8.30 till 12.00. The number of children varies between 15 and 20. The children have a Pakistani, Indian, Turkish or Moroccan background. Their caregivers are four apprentices, who have the same ethnic backgrounds as the children, but no experience or training as caregivers. They are appointed through an employment strategy, in this case mainly for unemployed youngsters, to obtain working experience during a seven month period. Their work is coordinated by one of the teachers of the language courses. In this way, the child centre supports ethnic minority parents and youngsters who gain experience and improve their future chance of finding paid work. Each morning between 8.30 and 9.00, the parents, mainly mothers, are together with their children. They sing and play together. This is done to teach the mothers how to sing and play with their children, assuming that this will contribute to their children's development. It is hoped that it will also give mothers the skills and motivation to play and sing at home.

Sweden

In Sweden, we visited two child-care centres. The first, in Södertalje near Stockholm, was an open preschool for parents and 0–7-year-old children. The other, in Göteborg, was a preschool for 1–7-year-olds. Both centres had one important characteristic in common. The staff put much energy in making the children's experiences, skills and knowledge the central element in the curriculum or activities. In the open preschool, this meant that activity planning had to be achieved almost on a day to day basis. In the other centre, staff were also very flexible, but they had instituted an observation period in August, to make a year plan adapted to a particular group of children. Consistent with this adaptive strategy were the many expeditions and trips that were organised for the children and parents. The staff argued that by making sure that activities are interesting to children, and within their capabilities in terms of skills and knowledge, the activities will have a developmentally enriching effect. Children were not forced to participate in such activities. They were allowed to engage in alternative activities. In case they did not take the initiative to find other activities, the caregivers helped them to find an alternative interesting activity. Such flexibility in planning did not have a negative impact on the orderliness of the activities.

To keep track of children's growth, staff of Vintersvädersgatan kept records of each child. We stress this characteristic, because staff described this approach as being partly the consequence of working with parents and children of different cultural backgrounds. Differences in interests, skills and knowledge between children are enormous, and need to be observed and recorded.

The centre in Södertalje is a child-care centre for mother and child. The centre is open from 8.30 till 15.30. Parents can come in whenever they want, but the two caregivers urge them to come before 10.00. The average number of children in the group is 23 in the morning, and 9 in the afternoon. Since it is an open preschool, the number of parents and children may vary daily. Ninety per cent of parents and children have an Assyrian background, as has one of the caregivers. The other 10% is Swedish. Parents play with the children, sing together and listen to stories. They also prepare fruit and drinks for the children and clean the tables. By helping and observing, they learn about how to educate their children. Parents are not constantly involved with children. The parents may sit together and drink their coffee, talking about their children or other topics that are important to them. They may also ask the caregivers for advice or just chat a little. For parents, the centre is a meeting place, where they can learn a lot from other mothers and from staff.

Both caregivers stated that they don't see it as their task to tell parents how they should educate their children at home, but they forbid the mothers to use corporal punishment when they are in the centre. They also teach parents that it is not bad for a child, or of themselves, when they don't provide their child with everything he or she demands.

On two afternoons, some of the mothers have a Swedish language class. The children are then supervised by the two caregivers. In the centre, mothers and children can speak Assyrian. Sometimes, the Assyrian caregiver joins in.

The centre in Göteborg is for children whose parents are employed. The centre is open between 6.15 and 18.00. Sixty per cent of the 55 children attending the centre have a Vietnamese, Turkish, Serbian or Hungarian cultural background. The only information which is of interest from a multicultural education viewpoint is that, during two afternoons, the 5–7-year-olds have a home language assistant who comes to class and engages in activities with children of a particular language group. Originally this measure was introduced for all children, but recently the government, for budgetary reasons, changed the financial facilitation. The centre has home language assistants for all groups.

Belgium

We visited two kindergartens, each of which was linked to a special support group. The kindergartens are part of a primary school with children aged 2–5 years. All young children in this age range are free to attend a kindergarten. The government and communities are required to provide enough places. The kindergartens are open between 8.45 and 15.15. Some children attend the centre only in the morning.

We visited a kindergarten in Lanklaar, which is supported by a project group 'family and school', and a kindergarten in Genk, which is supported by an in-service training group.

The kindergarten in Lanklaar is attended by some 60 children. Twenty three of these children have a Moroccan, Turkish, Italian, Spanish or Greek cultural background. The children are grouped in three age groups: 2–3, 3–4 and 4–5 years. Each group of about 20 children has one caregiver. For a few hours a week, the children engage in special language activities with a first language assistant. The rooms are rather exceptional. Much energy has been put into giving the rooms a multicultural ethos. Not only have the staff used Moroccan and Turkish wall displays, but they also decorated a little corner for Islamic worship, used as a place for silence and meditation by all children. Before entering the corner, the children have to take off their shoes. Apart from this corner, there are also the more common Western activity corners.

The project group family and school supports the kindergarten through three kinds of activities. First, they train the caregivers in monitoring and registering children's development through the use of tests and observation. Caregivers also are instructed how to use differentiation strategies. The combined use of monitoring and differentiation allows caregivers to adapt their programme to children's developmental needs. Second, they organise group meetings for parents. The group meetings take place in school and are held about six times a year. So far, about 50% of mothers have participated in the meetings. These meetings have several functions:

(1) providing a safe and enjoyable place were mothers can make friends, and speak about anything they feel like;
(1) informing parents about school, child development, care and education;
(3) making parents aware of their own education and the value of education for other activities in life.

Some topics discussed include games and play materials for children, punishing and rewarding children, and children living in different cultures. Third, the project group invites parents to participate in an enrichment programme. Once every two weeks, a mother comes to school during school hours. She and her child are instructed on how to work or play with a selected set of materials which are deemed to stimulate a child's cognitive development. After a short instruction period, the mother–child dyad may work or play together for 30 minutes. Mothers learn how to stimulate the child to concentrate, and how to give corrective and positive feedback. At the end of the session, the dyads receive new tasks which they may use at home. The type of tasks is similar to those tasks that children engage in at the kindergarten. An extra activity concerns Dutch language courses for immigrant women.

All these activities are meant to contribute directly or indirectly to children's development, and clearly reflect the notion that the development of children is the shared responsibility of parents and school. The values that are at the very heart of the activities, however, are more Western-type educational values than Mediterranean. More than other approaches to parent involvement described thus far, the families are invited to adopt these values as guiding principles in their educational activities.

The kindergarten in Genk also has three groups. Nearly 90% of children have a non-Belgian cultural background, mostly Turkish. The staff strongly perceives the kindergarten as an important step in children's development preparing them for their school career. The director explicitly stated that, although they had decorated the rooms with pictures representing other cultures and had books and play materials allowing children to experience other cultures, he saw this as rather superficial and hardly as an expression of multicultural education. The young children are not really aware of culture and cultural differences. Like all children, they have to learn basic social, cognitive, linguistic and motor skills. The class of the 2–3-year-olds had a Turkish speaking assistant to facilitate children's transition from home to school. Most Turkish children don't understand Dutch. First language instruction, however, is clearly not an important focus for the school. Instead, especially in the kindergarten, much attention is given to learning Dutch. In small groups, children have special language lessons from a language teacher. This teacher also advises the caregiver how to stimulate children's language development, mainly their vocabulary development.

As in Lanklaar, caregivers use a monitoring system to follow children's development and detect developmental or learning problems. In case problems arise, children get extra help, either in the class by the caregiver or via an assistant or outside the class by the language teacher or staff from an educational support centre.

Other initiatives in this school concern staff and the parents. The school promotes its staff's knowledge about Turkish culture in a very pleasant and probably very effective way. The whole team was preparing for two weeks visit to Turkey. Apart from this, all caregivers make home visits once a year. These have the combined function of school promotion/recruitment, informing parents about the Belgian school system and becoming informed about the home lives of children and their parents.

The school works together with a centre for adult education, which organises Dutch language courses and literacy courses in Turkish in the school. During the courses, parents are also informed about schools and Belgian educational principles. The topics are very much the same as those used for the group meetings in Lanklaar.

In the past, the school experienced a problem with parents who did not bring their children on time. The school organised meetings and showed videos to explain to parents that, for the good of their children, they should bring the child before 8.45. However, these activities were not effective. The team then decided to close the gate at 8.45. At first, parents were annoyed, but after a while they all made sure that they brought their child before 8.45. This seems a rather rigid and authoritarian policy, but an effective one. On the other hand, the school is clearly motivated to facilitate parental cooperation. The school has its own childminder, who can take care of schoolchildren and their brothers and sisters in cases of emergency (i.e. when parents cannot look after the children). This childminder is available between 7.00 and 18.00, but sometimes parents call on her in the middle of the night. As the director said: 'Working in a multicultural setting is very much a game of give and take'.

Germany

In Germany, we visited a kindergarten for 3–6-year-old children in Duisburg. Thirty per cent of the children had a Turkish cultural background. This centre had few specific activities or characteristics that created progressive examples of a multicultural approach, with one exception. Our visit was one month after the murder of five Turks in Solingen by youngsters with Nazi sympathies. Staff was shocked by what had happened. Together with the children, they had tried to express their feelings on a wall poster expressing the equality of children and their right of care, security and respect, irrespective of their ethnicity or colour. A clear political statement, expressed by children and staff and was visible to all visitors to the centre.

Spain

In Spain we visited a child-care centre in Barcelona for 41 gypsy children between 6 months and 3 years, and to a centre with a mixed Spanish, Moroccan, Filipino and Latin American population of 72 0–4-year-old children.

The first centre is in a small neighbourhood where only gypsies live and was started in the 1960s by a gypsy woman who came to live in the city. Currently, the centre is incorporated in the municipally funded system of day-care facilities.

The centre is open between 8.00 and 17.30 and has four groups; one for babies between 6 and 12 months, one for 1–2-year-old children, and two groups for the 2–3-year-olds. Each group has two caregivers, one starts at 8.00 and ends at 14.00. The other starts at 11.30 and ends at 17.30.

Since people marry young in the neighbourhood and teenage pregnancy is quite common, the parents of the children who attend the centre at the moment are well known by more than half of the staff (who have worked for more than fifteen years in this centre). They have known the parents as children who themselves attended the centre. The centre compensates for very basic limitations in its clientele's home care skills and education. The staff try to educate the young parents, but in a necessarily modest way, because the gypsies don't want the staff to direct their lives. The centre gives, and the parents mainly take. The centre has adapted in an effective manner to this principle. Instead of instructing parents in a direct way, the staff give them videos on which the parents can see their children and observe what kind of food is being prepared in the centre, how the children eat and how the staff change nappies. While enjoying looking at what their children do in the centre, the parents also learn basic rules of hygiene and child care.

With regard to language there is a difference between staff meetings, where Catalan is spoken, and contacts with children and parents, where Castilian is being used. An experiment in which staff spoke Catalan to the children as a preparation for the primary school (as Catalan is the language of instruction), was stopped when caregivers found out that the children no longer expressed themselves well in either language. The gypsies in the neighbourhood speak Castilian with some Calo as their home-language.

The second centre is located in the heart of the city and its opening times and staffing are comparable to the first centre's. In the sixties, many people from Spanish regions (such as, Andalusia, Estremadura and Galicia) came to Barcelona and it is estimated that, in the barrio, 50% of the population uses Catalan and another 50% Castilian as their home-language. One has to bear this in mind when being informed that 75% of the children who attend the centre are Spanish.

This percentage seems to indicate that it is a rather homogeneous group of children, but in reality, Spain is very much a multicultural society. The remaining 25% are immigrant children coming from Morocco, the Philippines and Peru. The number of immigrant children in the centre is increasing. The immigrant children add to the already broad variety of cultures in the centre. The centre has few special activities or a special approach for these immigrant children. The multicultural approach of this centre was described by the director as an effort to give all children the same effective care.

The centre has a clear and strict language policy. All children should learn Catalan, because that is the language they need in the primary school. No attempts were made to stimulate the development of children's home language.

The staff tried to maintain good relationships with parents. One of the strategies they used was with a notebook for every child. Staff wrote every day in the notebook what the child had achieved, whether he or she had slept and eaten well, how many times they had changed nappies etc. This note book was kept in the children's backpack so that parents could read it and also could write in it.

France

In France, we visited a 'halte garderie', a play group for 0–2-year-old children in Alès and an 'ecole maternelle', a kindergarten for 2–6-year-olds in Aulnay-sous-Bois.

The centre in Alès is open on Monday, Tuesday, Thursday and Friday between 8.30 and 11.45 and between 13.30 and 16.45. In every session, there is a maximum of ten children. The children attend the centre for two sessions or more. The centre is attended mainly by children whose parents were born in Northern Africa. The caregiver is Algerian. Originally, the centre functioned somewhat like the preschool in Södertalje in Sweden, but the municipality forced the staff to separate the education and care for children from the education and training of the mothers. Parents, however, are still very much involved in the centre's activities. Some of them bring their children and stay to play with them. Others join in when the children have outings. Such outings often have educational value for the children and the mothers. They may visit, for instance, a kindergarten, that prepares children and mothers for the elementary school. Once a week, the staff have a meeting to discuss educational matters, and this is also meant as a meeting to plan forthcoming activities. Parents are encouraged to take part in these meetings and some do. The centre also organises weekly group meetings for parents. The parents may themselves propose what they would like to talk about, or the centre staff prepare a topic for discussion. Apart from the explicit educational goal of such meetings, they clearly have a function of offering an enjoyable opportunity to chat with other women on important and less important things. The centre encourages parents as well as their children to speak their first language. Story telling and music are important ingredients in the centre's programme. These are used to give children and parents the feeling that people from a variety of cultural backgrounds can enjoy stories and music from other cultures.

The kindergarten in Aulnay-sous-Bois is open between 8.30 and 16.00. Some children stay on in the creche until 18.00. We visited the group for the two-year-olds and the group for the three-year-old children. Each group has about 25 children of which 80% have a non-French cultural background (mainly North African countries). Each group has a caregiver and an assistant. The assistant's tasks mainly centre on physical care.

The parents who bring their children may stay the first 30 minutes of the day. The caregivers informed us that they have no specific multicultural approach. However, because they work with immigrant children, they put extra energy into preparing children for primary school. Apart from ample attention for the French language, this is also evident from activities aimed at developing children's literacy and numeracy skills.

Staff's Goals for ECCE and Multicultural Education

To get a better idea about the type of educational goals that are central to multicultural education for young children we asked staff of the centres to rate ECCE goals. Twelve directors were asked to rate the importance of eight general goals, and they and 24 caregivers were also asked to rate the importance of nine possible goals of multicultural education. These have previously been listed in Chapter 3. Interviewees were requested to only rate those goals that were relevant to their contexts.

General goals

One director was the opinion that preparing children for primary school and the transmission of values and standards did not relate to the general goals of a child centre. Another director stated that providing good care was not a general educational goal. The three most important goals mentioned were:

(1) G5: Stimulate children's development.
(2) G2: Provide a safe and familiar environment for children.
(3) G8: Stimulate children to play together and to know each other better.

The two least popular general goals were:

(7) G4: Detect developmental problems in children.
(8) G3: Prepare children for primary school.

The higher priorities reflect the notion that child centres should stimulate the development of the whole child, not just cognitive aspects, and the low priorities show the almost general reluctance to follow a strict programmed approach, either geared at preparing for a primary school or geared to a notion of developmental tasks that allow staff to detect developmental problems.

Goals for multicultural education

The top three rated multicultural goals were:

(1) M4: Encourage a positive attitude towards representatives of other cultures by teaching children values and standards reflecting respect and acceptance.
(2) M5: Encourage cooperation and playing together by children from different cultural backgrounds.
(3) M2. Encourage a positive self image in ethnic minority children.

The lowest rated multicultural goals were:

(8) M6: Stimulate ethnic minority children's development and prepare them for primary school.
(9) M7: Prevent deprivation in ethnic minority children.

Five interviewees were the opinion that M6 has nothing to do with multicultural education and seven said the same for M7.

The top three multicultural goals are somewhat surprising after observing the practice of multicultural education, since we rarely found the means to accomplish these goals. Perhaps wall displays, listening to music and stories from a variety of cultures and the use of the children's first language are seen as such means, or, more implicitly, the simple fact that children from different cultural backgrounds meet in the centre.

The bottom two multicultural goals are comparable to the bottom two of the general goals. In the rejection of a programmatic approach, no exception is made for ethnic minority children. In England, this notion was fiercely stated by some interviewees, who suggested that these goals would be discriminatory or racist. Nevertheless, some centres, for instance in Belgium and France, had curricula aimed at precisely these goals, arguing that ethnic minority children need a good preparation for primary school.

We encountered a comparable inconsistency between goals and means concerning the development of children's first or second language proficiency. Such goals didn't find a prominent place in interviewees' judgement, whereas the corresponding language practices in the centres in England, Sweden, Denmark, Belgium and France were presented as characteristics of a multicultural approach. These inconsistencies are not simply due to our methodological approach to ascertaining the importance of goals in particular centres. Within all countries and within all centres, we find these same inconsistencies.

Goal Preferences in the Netherlands and Abroad

In the third chapter, we presented information on the goal preferences of Dutch centre staff. This chapter can therefore continue by comparing what we observed in other parts of Europe with the Netherlands. The results concern generalised findings. Individual centres' goal preferences may be quite different from this overview.

The top three general goals in the Netherlands were also, although in a slightly different order, the top three in the other countries. At number one in the Netherlands came 'provide a safe and familiar environment for children', which ranked two in the centres abroad. In second place, in the Netherlands, came the goal 'Stimulate children to play together and learn to know each other better'. Abroad this ranked third place. 'Stimulate children's development' ranked third in the Netherlands and first abroad. Both in the Netherlands and abroad, interviewees agreed that to 'prepare children for primary school' and 'detect developmental problems' were less important, and less essential goals for ECCE in centres.

We also asked the interviewees to rank goals specific to multicultural education. Here the unanimity between centres in the Netherlands and centres abroad was somewhat less clear cut. 'Encourage a positive self image in ethnic minority children' ranked number one in the Netherlands and number three in centres abroad. The goal 'Encourage a positive attitude towards representatives of other cultures by teaching children values and standards reflecting respect and acceptance' took first place in centres abroad, but had fourth place in the Netherlands. 'Encourage the cooperation and playing together by children of different cultural backgrounds' ranks high with Dutch as well as other European staff, coming third in the Netherlands and second in centres abroad. The most striking difference concerns the goal 'Prevent deprivation in ethnic minority children'. This goal had the lowest possible position (ninth) with staff abroad, but came in second position in the Netherlands. This high rank in the Netherlands, however, is due to a selective response. Most interviewees in the Netherlands were the opinion that this goal is not typical of multicultural education. Many simply excluded it from the ranking task. The interviewees who included it, ranked it high.

Both Dutch interviewees and interviewees from abroad deemed the following goals unimportant for multicultural education:

- Stimulate ethnic minority children's development and prepare them for primary school.
- Pay due attention to differences in food and sleeping habits and hygiene.
- Give children knowledge about different cultures.

Concluding Remarks

Multicultural education in centres for early childhood education and care affects both children and parents. As to the children, most centres encourage the development of children's first language (England, Sweden, Denmark, Belgium, Spain and France). They do this to smooth the transition from home to centre and to give the children a feeling of security and acceptance. The same reasoning is behind room layout, wall displays and the presence of non-indigenous staff. Other centres (England and Sweden) argue that, the children's first language, is helpful to their cognitive development. Second language teaching also is an important aspect of multicultural education (England, Belgium, Sweden, Spain, France). In our reporting thus far we haven't addressed caregiver child interaction styles, whether caregivers spoke a lot with children, listened to them and encouraged them to speak. We observed in some centres very responsive caregivers, and in others, caregivers who rushed around, very occupied by organisational activities. We visited centres with a 1:15 caregiver child ratio, where the caregivers were still available to all children and created a safe and exciting shelter for all children. We also visited centres with a 1:2 ratio where children felt lost between many adults and didn't find the interest, patience and security needed for engaging in enriching communication and activities. Several centres stress the need for extra attention to children's cognitive development (England and Belgium). The English nursery class was the only centre with a well defined curricular and didactic approach. Staff followed the High/Scope model (Weikart, 1987) with the 'plan–do–review' principle. Extra attention for children's cognitive development and attention to second language learning are kinds of prevention strategies to prevent later school dropout. Two centres had an explicit anti-racist policy and one, the German, a more implicit policy. In the latter, however, this had clear implications for children's activities, whereas in the others, the practical implications for the children were not so evident.

Staff of some centres clearly articulated that multicultural education with children refers more to the presence of children and staff with a variety of cultural backgrounds than to specifically planned activities. Simply giving the children equal treatment is enough, or as a director said, 'These children are not aware of differences, and why make them aware of them. They do everything together and all have to learn so many other basic things'.

In most centres, multicultural approaches include the education of parents. Some child centres were started to allow mothers to participate in activities in community centres, from simple social meetings to language courses. Most centres aim to influence parents' way of caring and educating their children. This is achieved by a variety of ways, from mothers who participate in the centre, to home visits through courses and to giving parents videos and pictures. Some are very explicit in doing this (Belgium), others are very modest (Spain) and some deny, but still do it (Sweden). Some centres restrict their attempts to aspects of care, food, hygiene and health, others want parents to support their children's development by playing and talking to them. In this latter option, cognitive enrichment is generally the goal.

With regard to centre–parent relationships, we have two comments. The first is that centres rarely try to find out what are parents educational values and how the parents prefer the centre to support these values. Staff talk to parents about food and sleeping habits, and sometimes about punitive measures (Sweden), but little more. Some interviewees stated that their preference is to avoid conflicts about values, rather than open discussion about them trying to reach a consensus. The general attitude may be summarised in the notion 'as long as parents don't complain, we have a consensus'.

The second comment regards anti-racism. As stated before, some centres had a clear anti-racism policy. However, none of the centres tried to make anti-racism an issue in their attempts to educate parents. Parents are used as important instruments in attempts to create a linguistically and cognitive rich environment for their children, but no one centre showed them how they are instrumental in their children's attitudes towards other cultures and how they can help in avoiding discriminating or being the victims of discrimination. As Allport (1979) indicated, parents are children's natural partners in matters of prejudice, racism and discrimination: '...there is no society on earth where the children are thought to belong to the ethnic and religious group of their parents. By virtue of kinship, the child is expected to take on the prejudices of his parents, also to become the victim of whatever prejudice is directed against his parents' (p. 291).

If eradicating or avoiding racism and discrimination is an important goal, and we argue it is, educationists should educate children's parents to play an important role in the eradication of prejudice and racism in children.

In the introduction we stated that this chapter had a double function: to show the comparability of the situation in ECCE and multicultural education in ECCE institutions in a variety of European countries, and clarify that the way centres operate in the different countries is influenced by particular contexts. Such context relatedness can be clarified further. We take the nursery class in England as an example. Important ingredients of such as educational approach were the attention to children's first and second language development, a clearly structured cognitively-oriented curriculum, and attempts to give parents the means to support children's development in a manner consistent with the centre's approach. Such attention to children's language development goes back to a Local Educational Authority's policy measure, as do the attempts to establish good contacts with the children's homes. The choice of a cognitively oriented curriculum seemed, at least partly, inspired by the broader educational context. The nursery was part of a primary school. We found comparable school-like approaches in other preschools that were part of a primary school (e.g. in Belgium).

The commonalities between the Dutch centres and the centres abroad became particularly clear at the level of staff goal preferences. Goal preferences abroad and in the Netherlands are largely comparable. This is clear for the favourite goals, but even more for the goals staff deem unimportant for either ECCE in general or for multicultural education in ECCE. Drawing children's attention to cultural differences between children and adults, and teaching cognitive skills and knowledge, are not popular with child-care centre staff. They don't specify what they want to achieve with children. Staff seems to make an exception to learning values reflecting respect for and acceptance of ethnic minorities.

5 Models for Multicultural Education

The descriptions in Chapters 3 and 4 do not provide a clear notion about what constitutes multicultural education in ECCE. Centres vary quite extensively in their choice of goals and means which form the heart of the centres' multicultural approaches. Centres mostly prefer a general approach, an approach stressing that goals are for all children. Specific approaches, that imply specific means and goals for particular groups of children (e.g. migrant children) are less popular with centre staff, in the Netherlands as well as in other European countries. In this chapter, we therefore need to clarify further an answer to the question 'What is the state of multicultural education in ECCE?' We portray our research information in terms of the four models for multicultural education in primary education presented in Chapter 1:

(1) submersion in mainstream language and culture;

(2) facilitation of a transition between home culture and mainstream culture and language;

(3) changing the mainstream culture and language use within the centre;

(4) influencing ethnic relationships (varying from mutual understanding between people to prevention of institutional racism).

In this chapter we mainly analyse information about multicultural education ECCE from the Netherlands, since we have more detailed information about the situation in the Netherlands than in the other countries. In the next section, however, we shall use examples of educational practices both in the Netherlands and abroad.

In the preceding chapter we presented evidence for the comparability of the situation in the Netherlands and other European countries. Hence, we assume that our findings for the Netherlands are largely valid for other, neighbouring, countries as well.

Models as Ideal Types

Models can be presented as ideal types. An ideal type is specified in terms of an ideology of achievable goals and the means needed to attain those goals. Descriptions of practice can be compared to these ideal types. Such a comparison may reveal that a centre uses various ideologies, each corresponding to a separate model, and each model is represented by different staff members. The comparison also might reveal that the means that are used in a centre correspond to different models. Reflection on the use of various ideologies or a variety of means corresponding to several models may be a first step towards a more unified, coherent and rational approach by a centre. Working with goals and means from different models is not a problem provided that the models do not conflict . In reality, Model 1 (submersion in mainstream culture and language) clearly conflicts with Model 2 (facilitating the transition between home culture and mainstream culture) and Model 3 (changing the mainstream culture). However, using conflicting ideologies and means, as some centres do, is a serious problem. In such a situation, a centre 'preaches' something different from what it practices.

In this section, we give a short idealised, but typical description of each model in terms of ideology and means. As to the means, we distinguish between environmental adaptation, group composition, activities for children, the caregiver's role and parental participation.

Model 1: Submersion in the mainstream language and culture

Central to this model is the notion of the same goals, the same approach, and the same means being applied to all children. The values and goals guiding the organisation and activities in a centre are typical of a common-sense notion about what good quality care and education is for Dutch infants. Immigrant children may receive some extra attention, but this is aimed at facilitating or accelerating their adaptation to general rules in the centre and to using the Dutch language. The children's cultural background plays no role in such extra attention. Facilitation or acceleration of adaptation is necessary because the staff deem children's home education less adequate as a preparation for children's functioning in the centre and later in school.

A belief in the same goals, same approach and same means for all children can easily be confused with an equal opportunities approach. Although these two approaches are not necessarily in conflict with each other, one should keep in mind that using the first approach might lead to a neglect or depreciation of children's cultural skills and knowledge, such as their home language, stories and games that they have learned and played at home. This does not provide an equal opportunities system.

In a centre led by this model, no attempt is made to adapt the rooms or the play materials and books to the presence of immigrant children. Staff generally argue that materials are chosen because they contribute to a developmentally enriching environment for all children.

Staff try to avoid a large influx of immigrant children, and have no special recruitment policy favouring immigrant children. Too high a proportion of immigrant children could jeopardise the use of a general approach. The immigrant children might need extra attention such that Dutch children might receive less attention. If Dutch children are in the majority, the Dutch language will be the common language of the centre. Attending the centre allows the immigrant children to have ample contact with this language, such that individual language shift from the immigrant to the national language can occur.

As to activities for children, no attention is paid to cultural differences between children. No attempt is made to inform children about habits, games, knowledge and the languages that are typical of different cultural groups. Discrimination, however, is forbidden. Instead, there is a rule of good manners and peaceful coexistence, which holds for all children, irrespective of their ethnic origins.

Immigrant children, like other children in need, may receive extra attention if staff perceives this is necessary. Such immigrants may have language problems in Dutch, or other social and emotional problems. The solution to the language problem is twofold. First, the centre will try to teach Dutch as a second language and create opportunities for children to use this language. Second, staff will advise parents to use Dutch in the home, for instance, by reading Dutch story books. No caregiver is allocated a special role as regards immigrant parents. Hence, there is no special need to recruit immigrant caregivers.

Parent involvement is deemed important so long as parents respect what is achieved in the centre and comply with staff wishes for help either in the centre, or at home (for instance, the use of the Dutch language). Parent involvement primarily means that parents facilitate but do not formulate the care and education policy in the centre. Parents are not allowed to get in a position where they claim educational changes that would imply an adaptation of the centre's organisation and activities to the presence of children and parents with a variety of cultural backgrounds.

Model 2: Facilitation of the transition between home culture and mainstream culture and language

The starting point for this model is attention for the variety in children's cultural backgrounds. Immigrant children's transitions between different cultural settings, mainly centre and home, should be facilitated to avoid children feeling confused and insecure. The assumption is that immigrant children will probably experience these negative experiences if either their home does not prepare them for the centre, or a centre does not cater for their specific needs. Giving due attention to children's cultural background in the centre is seen as a means to smooth the transition. The centre may use special wall displays or play materials representing different ethnic groups and activities. The major goal, however, is to facilitate children's adaptation to mainstream rules, values and language.

Use of this model indicates that the centre's main concern is the care and education of immigrant children. The presence of Dutch children may be helpful in accomplishing this goal. Dutch children enable immigrant children to experience the majority language, culture and beliefs through informal play.

For the centre it is important to use care patterns that children are familiar with from the home situation. A centre might use special cots or slings to carry babies around. Furthermore, it is deemed very important that children can identify with images and themes in play materials, books, and wall displays. This will help them feel at ease and accepted, and it will encourage them to explore all the centre has to offer.

If the centre already has many immigrant children there is no need for a special recruitment strategy favouring immigrant children. Centres with few immigrant children, yet are sited in neighbourhoods with a large proportion of immigrant families, may start a special recruitment campaign.

The focus is on the relationship between the minority and majority culture, and the home and centre culture, and how to bridge the gap between the two. The model doesn't stress the importance of celebrating in a variety of cultural backgrounds. This means for instance that a centre will not invest much time and effort in informing children about a variety of cultures or in stimulating children to develop a positive attitude towards a variety of cultures. Centres might do so, but this is not a characteristic of the model. Prevention and remediation of developmental and learning problems is important as is the creation of an environment in which children can develop first language skills. Parents are given advice to stimulate children's first language development. To achieve an assimilation goal, however, the centre tries to involve immigrant children in conversations in Dutch language. The centre will monitor the developmental progress of each child and seek possibilities to link the outcomes with the activity plan or with special, extra developmental activities. Although play is seen as important to children, a centre working according to this model stresses the importance of good preparation for school and includes systematic, caregiver-guided learning activities in the curriculum, for instance language lessons or short, small-group game sessions to stimulate children's phonological awareness.

Since attention to children's first language development is important, the centre will try to recruit staff who are proficient in immigrant children's first language. Immigrant caregivers also have special functions with immigrant parents. They can act as interpreters and facilitators. Moreover, such immigrant caregivers would function as an information source about children's home cultures for the benefit of the rest of the staff.

Parents' involvement is very important in this model. First, parents can inform staff about the care patterns that children are acquainted with and about any peculiarity of the child that is important to understand the way the child behaves in the centre. Second, parents can help to facilitate the transition by stimulating children's first language development at home, or by participating in home intervention programmes aimed at developmental enrichment. Centre staff might decide to link with a centre for adult education and encourage parents to start a course. The idea is that additional parent education will contribute to creating a developmentally enriching environment at home.

Staff will try to be as responsive as possible to parents' wishes or claims for change, so long as these changes will facilitate children's transition between home and centre culture and contribute to reaching the major goal: adaptation to Dutch culture.

Model 3: Changing the mainstream culture in the centre

This model focuses on the notion that any culture has elements that are functional and valuable for other cultures as well. It is important to let persons, in this case mainly children, experience a variety of cultures, allowing them to choose from each culture a unique mosaic. The value of some elements of Dutch culture might be questioned, for instance, emphasis on the individual achievement and autonomy. Such a cultural emphasis may lead to feelings of frustration and a perception of a consequent underdevelopment of social responsibility.

Model 3 clearly differs from the preceding models as it focuses on the variety of cultures and cultural experiences, instead of a disassociation between two cultures. For both Dutch and other children, it is important to experience a variety of cultures, to overcome feelings of strangeness, and to use not just one, but a variety of cultures for full social development. The goal is the development of a new cosmopolitan culture, with integrated elements from a variety of cultures. Culture is taken to be a dynamic, changing entity. Cultural change often results from necessary adaptations to changes in living conditions (e.g. linked with migration). To a limited extent, cultural change may also result from contact between cultures and re-evaluations of the functionality of elements from particular cultures. Recently, for instance, a discussion was commenced in the Netherlands as to whether it still makes sense for all to celebrate traditional Christian holy days. Whit Monday, for instance, is a free day for all Dutch people, and is appreciated as a day off, but is not really perceived as a holy day. The possibility of cultural change through contact between cultures and through a re-evaluation of the functionality of elements from cultures is central to Model 3.

A centre working according to this model would at first use a variety of care patterns from different cultures. A process of selection and integration of care patterns, eventually may lead to less variation as standard practices are established. From available well understood child care, staff choose what they deem best. This, however, only happens if the variety of cultures represented in the centre is relatively stable. If a centre has a steadily changing set of cultures, it will be more difficult to achieve stability and integration. Food and play materials in the centre will reflect and exemplify such cultural variety.

A prerequisite for practising this model is the presence of children from a variety of cultures. Otherwise it may become a quaint, superficial and artificial exercise. The centre may have a special recruitment strategy to attract children from a variety of cultures and to maintain that variety. A centre with mainly or only non-white children may try to recruit Dutch children to add to the cultural variety.

Staff will explore ways to transmit knowledge about different cultures. To do this they may select games, songs and stories from different cultures and try to involve children in dialogues, drama and role playing allowing them to show each other the knowledge and skills they have learned at home. Developmental and learning problems may receive little attention. Such individual problems are conceived differently in different cultures. If staff pay attention to such personal problems, they may feel themselves trapped in defining problems mainly from a Western perspective, stressing cognitive problems and problems with Dutch language proficiency. A multilingual approach is typical of this model. All children will be expected to become bilingual. All Dutch and Turkish children, for instance, will learn both Turkish and Dutch.

It is important to employ caregivers representing different cultures. They are important information sources and role models. More important than anything else, however, is that caregivers have an open attitude towards other cultures. They should respect and positively value cultural variety and show this by learning and using skills and knowledge from other cultures. They themselves have to cross cultural boundaries.

Parent involvement is highly valued in this model. Parents can provide information about their culture and they can assist caregivers in realising cultural diversification in the centre. Moreover they, as well as the professional educators themselves, can function as safeguards against ethnocentrism.

Centres working towards this model have to be very cautious of the risk of identifying culture too much with folklore and depicting culture more as something stable and eternal rather than as something dynamic and developmental. This could easily result in a curriculum that lacks realism. It isolates cultures and their representatives. Instead, a multicultural curriculum should build bridges.

This model is rarely practised in the Netherlands, probably because it is difficult to achieve, since people are generally reluctant to cross cultural boundaries. Most people value the sense of belonging to an identifiable culture and having a clear a social identity. Social identity is partly defined in terms of group affiliation. A positive social identity often goes together with favouring one's own group whereas other groups are depreciated. This may lead to social competition and rejection between groups (Van Oudenhoven, 1990). People won't easily give up a feeling of belonging and a positive social identity to change it for something which they don't experience as theirs, about which they know very little, and which they even might see as something of low status, of little value and rejectable (cf. Smeyers, 1991).

As was stated earlier, parent involvement is highly valued in this model. In Chapter 3 however, we showed that few caregivers make home visits, which is an effective means to get to know families better. In part, this may be explained by a fear of strangeness, which is reinforced if no (or badly organised) visits are made. Caregivers won't overcome this fear unless they try to learn as much as possible from the experiences of others (e.g. should I take off my shoes; what to do when they ask me repeatedly whether I would like some more tea or more sweets, while I am on a diet, or when I actually don't like the tea or the sweets), and prepare the families for their visit (informing parents that a home visit will be made, why it is important, what it will involve, whom the caregiver hopes to meet, and of course making appointments). However, staff fear is probably not the only reason for a lack of home visits. Some parents will indicate to the visitor that they don't appreciate a home visit. These families may experience home visits, or other attempts to stimulate parent involvement, as an intrusion to their private lives, or as some sort of control mechanism. Others, with a strong in-group orientation, will be afraid that other group members might see it as a rejectable, out-group behaviour. (Hewstone, 1989; Pettigrew, 1979; Tennekes, 1989).

Model 4: Influencing ethnic relationships

This model stresses mutual understanding, solidarity and respect between children from different cultures. Immigrant children should be proud of themselves and their culture. Prevention of prejudice and discrimination is also important in this model. A model centre will have an anti-racist policy. This will include strategies to inform parents about their role in the development and prevention of prejudice and discrimination in their children, and clear anti-racist rules operating in the centre in case parents experience prejudice and discrimination among their children.

A centre will try to select play materials, books and wall displays from a variety of cultures. These materials should not reflect ethnocentrism or discrimination. All children should equally feel at home and respected in the centre. Since the presence of children from a variety of cultures makes the task of mutual respect and understanding more possible, centres would normally try to create a multicultural population. A centre, however, would be hesitant in favouring particular groups, since this might be perceived as a form of discrimination. The presence of children from different cultures is not an absolute prerequisite for practising this model. If the centre's children are culturally homogeneous, a centre can use books, videos and other information to give children experience of other cultures. Apart from the moral implication that all children are equal, centre activities are aimed at children experiencing that it is fun to know other cultures. They should lose the feeling of strangeness in contact with people from other cultures, and the artifacts and activities that are characteristic of these cultures.

Staff will be hesitant in implementing special educational measures for immigrant children, for instance mother tongue tuition, or extra development-enriching activities, or to prevent learning problems. Individual children, who need extra help, get this help irrespective of their background.

The presence of immigrant staff is important, because it shows immigrant parents and children that their presence is normal and respected. All caregivers need to be sensitive to their own ethnocentrism as well as ethnocentrism in colleagues, parents and children. They need skills to educate about ethnocentrism and discrimination when conversing with parents and colleagues.

Parent involvement is important. Parents should help in the eradication of prejudice and discrimination in children. Other aspects of home education, such as language use and developmental stimulation, are seen as the parents' responsibility. The centre won't try to intervene. Immigrant parents' participation in parent meetings, parent committees or boards is ideally via a proportional representation.

The Models in Practice

In practice, one will rarely find a centre whose educational approach perfectly corresponds to one of the ideal types presented in the preceding section. Centres will correspond more or less to one of the models or to a combination. We tried to identify for each of the models a centre whose practices come closest to the ideal types.

In our study, Centre I is a representative of Model 1 (submersion in mainstream language and culture). Both the ideology and processes in this centre correspond to this model. A typical quotation from the interview with the coordinator was: 'Working here already means that you need extra skills and a special attitude, not particularly for immigrant children. We have so many children with behavioural problems. Each child is a person on his or her own. We don't like to categorise. Each morning we evaluate what children are doing in the group. We use multi-age groups, which is very stimulating for all children. Of course, we also evaluate whether children whose home language is not Dutch need extra attention. But, actually this is the same as we would do for any child. When you find out that a child has particular problems, a caregiver gives him special attention.'

We visited two centres abroad that were clearly representatives of Model 1: the centre in Barcelona with the Spanish, Moroccan, Filipino and Latin American population and the kindergarten at Aulnay-sous-Bois in France. Typical of both centres is the ample attention to children's mastery of the majority language.

Centre H is the best representative of Model 2 (facilitation of the transition between home cultures and mainstream culture and language). This centre has only Turkish children which underlines that Model 2 is not really concerned with a variety of cultures, but with the gap between minority and majority culture. Preparing children for primary school is important in this centre. The staff give children tasks to stimulate their cognitive and language development. This centre, however is not a pure representative of Model 2. Its centre staff stress the importance of a positive attitude towards cultural variety (Model 4). Moreover, although they stress children's smooth transition towards the majority culture, they are also in favour of a strong cultural maintenance policy (more characteristic of Model 3). This latter policy may be instrumental in achieving the transitional goal, but eventually, culture maintenance conflicts with adaptation to the majority culture if it is not restricted to the private sphere.

Of the centres we visited abroad, the nursery class visited in England is a representative of Model 2, although its staff were somewhat reluctant to link attention to learning problems with children's cultural background. Important ingredients of their educational approach were the attention to children's first and second language development, a clearly structured cognitively oriented curriculum and attempts to give parents the means to support children's development in a manner consistent with the centre's approach.

It was very difficult to find a centre representing Model 3 (changing the mainstream culture of, and language use within the centre). Nevertheless, some elements of this model are found in Centre A. The following quotations give an illustration: 'We tried to recruit children from all cultures represented in this neighbourhood'. And about parent involvement: 'The shared responsibility for children's education should receive more attention. We should try to find out what the elements are in each culture that are important for children's development. These elements from a variety of cultures should be integrated. At this moment, the influence of a variety of cultures is very limited. We should try to use them more as sources for constructing the best type of care and education for children from a broad variety of cultures.'

The centre uses songs and stories from a variety of cultures, and one of the caregivers uses foot massages common in some Surinamese groups. The centre, moreover, participates in a multilingual project. This project however, does not aim at making all children multilingual.

Centre J is a representative of Model 4 (influencing ethnic relationships). Typical quotations from the interviews are: 'Last week we had a Turkish snack. We tell children where it comes from and that people who originally lived there came to the Netherlands. Turkish children may look a bit different, and they may dress in other clothes than most Dutch children, but they play and move in the same way and they are as sweet as all other children'. 'We try to adapt our educational approach as well as possible to the educational approach at home. However, if parents have ideas that do not correspond to what we think is good for children, we respect parents' approach but won't adopt these ideas.'

As we shall see in the next subsection, many centres use elements from this model. However, none of the centres has a clear anti-racist policy, or tries to inform parents about the parents' role in the development of prejudice and discrimination in children.

For the third and fourth model, we found no clear representatives abroad. We saw, however, examples of good practice of elements of these models, for instance in anti-racist policies. The second centre we visited in England had a formal equal opportunities policy statement, addressing racism and discrimination. The centre in Scotland had an anti-racist policy with a clear rule as to what should happen in cases of discrimination in the centre. Such a statement or such a practice was not encountered in the Netherlands.

The conclusion is that the models presented are valuable to categorise multicultural practices in ECCE.

Centres and Models

The models may be used to describe, reflect on, and analyse multicultural education in nurseries and playgroups. In this section, we try to link all centres we visited in the Netherlands with the models that they represent. We show that this may lead to questions about change, and that the models have a use in evaluation.

In this chapter, we have distinguished ideology from means. Our classification illustrates how the models can be used, and how the use of the models as tools for describing and analysing centres may lead to suggestions for change.

Several centres use different ideologies and means from different models. In the introduction to this section, we suggested that this situation leads to problems if it concerns Model 1 together with either Model 2 or Model 3. No such problems were found, in practice. With the selection of means, however, problems were located in Centres A and B. This situation may occur when staff reflect too little on the relationship between ideology and means, and when a centre discusses its ideology but leaves the means more or less to the responsibility of individual caregivers.

Also problematic is the situation in Centre C. This centre contains two ideologies stressing the need of adaptation to children's cultural background, but the caregivers don't utilise the necessary means to realise the ideologies. This will impair the achievement of important goals and thus jeopardises the quality of this centre. Nine centres lack a clear and consistent pedagogical plan, which is respected and implemented by all caregivers. It goes almost without saying that, if all caregivers do not help achieve the same goals, goal realisation will not occur. Staff in these centres clearly need to discuss and reflect on their aims and strategies of action.

Staff of the other centres may evolve if they reflect more on their aims and goals, and the strategies to achieve these goals. Our models provide a stimulus for such reflection. A serious comparison of a centre's practices with the ideal types may also lead to the conclusion that the centre could develop its practice. For instance, staff of a centre in favour of Model 2 might become aware that they should monitor children's developmental progress in a systematic manner, in order to be better able to prepare children for school.

Table 5.1 Centres and the models they represent

Centre	Ideology	Means
A	3, 4	3, 1, 2
B	4, 2	1, 2
C	3, 4	1
D	1, 4	4
E	4	4
F	4, 2	2, 4
G	2	2
H	2, 4, 3	2
I	1	1
J	4	4

Conclusion

The four models we described in the first section provide a generalised description of current child-care practices and notions of multicultural education in early childhood education, and help in understanding the state of multicultural education in ECCE. In terms of ideologies or goals, most of the centres we visited stressed the importance of building positive relationships between children from different cultural and ethnic backgrounds, whereas very few promoted submersion in mainstream culture and language. In Chapters 3 and 4, we pointed out that centres are more in favour of a general approach to multicultural education. The classification of centres we visited, however, suggests that these centres have less problems with a specific approach (Model 2). They use it in combination with general approaches represented in Models 1, 3 and 4.

The models can have a normative function as well. Administrators and centre staff can use them as guides to a preferred new approach in their centre. Staff and administrators may judge that the present situation in their centre is represented best by, for instance Model 1, whereas they would prefer that it had more characteristics as depicted in Model 2. The models as ideal types may be used as tools for identifying what multicultural education in ECCE should look like.

6 Quality in Multicultural Education

In the preceding chapter, we argued that the four models for multicultural education may be used as an analytical tool for answering the question: 'What should multicultural education in ECCE look like?' In this chapter we try to find more specific answers to this question.

The starting point for this chapter is that the quality of education can only be evaluated if the goals to be achieved in education are first specified. In this chapter, we explore what goals are deemed important for multicultural education in ECCE and for ECCE in general. As discussed before, the quality of multicultural education in ECCE cannot be isolated from the general quality of ECCE.

Three parties are involved in discussions about goals: centre staff, parents and experts. In the Netherlands, only staff and parents are directly involved in deciding what goals are important. Experts have no direct role. We are nevertheless interested in their ideas, since they may have an important impact through textbooks, training and other means of conveying educational knowledge and skills to a wider audience. For each of these parties we can identify their goal preferences.

In Chapter 3, we have already presented centre staffs' preferences. We showed that, within centres, not all caregivers deem the same goals to be important, and in our presentation of conflicts between staff and parents in that same chapter, we saw that parents and staff may disagree about goals. Disagreement between persons involved in deciding what goals are important for ECCE and in multicultural education makes it very difficult, or impossible to decide what goals can be used for measuring the quality of such education. Explicit or tacit consensus between educators about important goals, is, at least in a democracy, a prerequisite for quality assessment.

A Search for Important Goals

Centre staff

We summarise the findings presented in Chapter 3 and 4 regarding the central goals of centre staff. Important goals for ECCE in general, about which caregivers seem to have a great deal of consensus, are:

(1) Provide an environment in which children are safe and feel secure.
(2) Stimulate children to cooperate and play together.
(3) Encourage children's development in general.

Caregivers also agree about at least one goal for multicultural education: encourage a positive attitude towards representatives of other cultures by teaching them values and standards reflecting respect and acceptance.

Far less agreement was found about the importance of attention to children's mother tongue, food and care related habits, a centres' role in preparing children for primary school, and in preventing learning problems.

Parents

Parents are generally seen, at least in the Netherlands, as the professional educators' natural partners in providing good high quality education for their children. If the centres' quality is not satisfactory, parents are the first to complain and to correct or improve the situation. We present some results from a recently conducted large scale survey (Terpstra, Van Dijke & Hermanns, 1994). The researchers did not include questions on playgroups, hence we restrict ourselves to nurseries. They used a representative sample of parents in the Netherlands.

Different perspectives on quality

Although originally designed for children whose parents were deemed incapable of raising their children themselves, nurseries are currently meant for parents who want (or need) to combine parenting with a career, or who value care centres as a quality supplement to a child's education, or simply as a relief giver. Parents not only have pedagogical interests in dealing with nurseries. When evaluating the quality of a centre, they may also be guided by concerns about their work, their career or simply their free time off. The work perspective is especially important for matters such as accessibility of the centre, the distance between home and the centre, the centre's opening hours, and the continuity of care in case a caregiver becomes ill.

Parents, particularly mothers, may experience conflicts between their aspiration to earn a good salary or building a professional career and their wish to be intensively involved in the education and development of their babies and toddlers. Such conflicts are particularly clear and acute when a child becomes ill. The child needs much attention when ill, but the employer doesn't allow the mother to stay home. Either feigning that she herself is ill or using her holidays is a practical solution to such a problem. This indicates that, while mothers are being encouraged to take up employment, the education of the children is still seen as their almost exclusive, responsibility. Most employers are still very reluctant or hesitant in facilitating mothers' attempts to combine a job and the education of their children.

Without specifying the perspectives from which they evaluate the quality of the child care, 85% of parents whose children attend a nursery are satisfied with the centre and deem this type of child care better than other arrangements. They say that, as compared to other arrangements, nurseries provide good conditions for children's social development. In nurseries, children can play together and they learn rules of social conduct. An important additional advantage is that nurseries guarantee continuity in care. If one of the professional educators is ill, another takes over. Parents are the opinion that nursery staff are very forthcoming in following parents' wishes about care-related activities such as bowel training, eating and sleeping. In other domains, for instance, curriculum matters or employment and recruitment policies, parents' wishes and opinions are taken into account far less, but parents are not really critical about this.

The researchers suggest that parents' lack of criticism doesn't typically correspond to conflicts they experience when sending their children to a nursery. Parents try to justify sending their child to a nursery, whereas underneath they are less sure whether it is the best thing for their child. Being concerned about the quality of nursery child care is, in a sense, pointless. Given the shortage of child places, parents don't really have a choice between good and bad, and better or worse nurseries. They are just lucky to find a place.

Parents' educational preferences

Asked how they think the atmosphere in the ideal nursery should be, more than half the parents answered that it should primarily be a cosy, loving and caring environment, where children feel relaxed, safe, secure and accepted. Parents appear to be describing an ideal home situation. In second place, they named characteristics such as consistency in caregivers' approach, tranquillity, and an enriching stimulating environment. Professionalism of staff, permissiveness towards children, hygiene and contacts between parents were among the other qualities mentioned by some parents. It is unclear whether most parents really think the latter qualities are less important, or that they perceive that the centres naturally cover these. The researchers drew an important conclusion. They state that parents are primarily interested in those qualities, summarised as creating an ideal home situation, qualities that are less tangible and are more difficult to influence through policy and training.

What would parents like caregivers to do with their children? From nine alternatives the parents choose (a) teaching rules of social conduct, (b) the stimulation of social development, and (c) stimulating children's fantasy and creativity as the three most important. From the same list, they picked alternatives that they deemed less important. Parents say that (d) teaching children world knowledge, and (e) giving them space and freedom for doing what they feel like, are of little importance. One goal is clearly least important: f) preparing children for primary school.

The parental goals identified so far all refer to ECCE in general. The researchers asked parents one question about multicultural education: whether they think that attention to different cultures represented in Dutch society is important. Sixty per cent of the parents said it is, whereas 13% deemed it unimportant.

From other studies (Eldering & Vedder, 1992; Pels, 1991, 1994; Van der Leij, 1991; Vedder, 1995), we know that immigrant parents in the Netherlands find it very important that their young children learn Dutch in nurseries and playgroups and receive an effective preparation for learning the basic skills for primary school (reading, writing, arithmetic). They are afraid that goals they deem even more important, such as respecting adults and obedience, might be undermined by the centres' attention for openness, free play, autonomy in making choices for activities, ways of addressing adults, a lack of discipline and a lack of punitive measures to order and control.

Experts

We sent 18 experts (See Appendix 1) a questionnaire inquiring about their opinion on:

- the desirable functions of child-care centres and multicultural education in the centres;
- the desirable goals for ECCE and multicultural education in ECCE.

Functions refer to broad goal domains that involve either children, parents or society, whereas goals refer to concrete activity domains for children.

The surveyed experts are policy makers, social scientists involved in early childhood education or multicultural education or managers in training centres, institutes for programme development or child-care centres. More information about the experts can be found in Appendix 1.

The function of child-care centres

Most experts stated that stimulating children's development in general is a major function of a child-care centre. Some experts are more specific in the kind of development that is important: the social development and the development of play is named by six experts, two point to the importance of stimulating cognitive development, and two experts mention the stimulation of independence and self confidence. The development of creative/artistic, linguistic and physical qualities are only mentioned once each by one expert.

In their answers, the experts sometimes emphasised additional aspects:

- A centre should not operate in isolation of familiar environments (i.e. family and community).
- It is important to respond to the needs of all children (i.e. their cultural and linguistic needs), and to utilise the qualities of the staff and to provide a stimulating curriculum.
- Extra stimulation for children is legitimate only if this corresponds to parents' wishes or is necessary because of children's handicaps.

Institutional child care has an important function for parents in that they offer the combined opportunity to have children and participate on the labour market. This was mentioned by seven experts. Another important function, according to six experts, is the support child-care centres can give to parents, whether this is by being a forum where parents can obtain educational questions with other parents or by being a place where they can get advice or can find some kind of help in raising their children. Four of the experts point to the partnership in education and care between parents and child-care centres; a partnership in which educational responsibilities are shared. Some experts believe that child-care centres have a function for parents in that they can offer something 'extra' beside the care and education given at home: for example more possibilities for developmentally enriching activities for the child, detecting developmental deviations, and providing a socially stimulating environment. Three experts implicitly or explicitly stated that child-care centres also have a responsibility towards parents. The centre should guarantee a secure environment where parents can bring their children in good trust.

The existence of child-care centres influences the emancipation of women. This social function was mentioned by six experts. Another important function is that through child-care centres, society can take part in the socialisation of children at an early age. More specifically, four experts mentioned that child-care institutions can stimulate and support the development of children at an early age, which in the long term will have an influence on children's school careers and later, functioning in society. Child-care centres can also have more idealistic functions in society. Early socialisation can contribute to diminishing social inequality and to an increase in individual self confidence and critical consciousness.

Goals for ECCE

Fifteen experts indicated which of the goals they deemed important for ECCE. The numbers between brackets refer to the number of experts choosing the mentioned goal.

(A) Prepare children for their future lives in general (10).
(B) Provide a familiar and stimulating environment for children (15).
(C) Provide good physical care for children (12).
(D) Encourage the development of children (14).
(E) Detect developmental deviations in children (9).
(F) Pay special attention to the prevention of deprivation in children (10).
(G) Prepare children for educational tasks in elementary school (7).
(H) Provide a stimulating language environment (14).
(I) Give children certain values and standards (11).
(J) Give children knowledge about the world around them (13).
(K) Make children familiar with other children (15).
(L) Make children familiar with other adults (15).
(M) Encourage a positive self-image in children (14).

All experts prioritised 'provide a familiar and stimulating environment for children,' 'make children familiar with other children,' and 'make children familiar with other adults' important tasks. 'Encourage the development of children,' 'provide a stimulating language environment,' and 'encourage a positive self-image in children' were also often seen as relatively important tasks. Least popular was the goal 'prepare children for elementary school'.

The experts disagree on the priority to be allocating to the following goals 'detect developmental deviations in children' and 'pay special attention to the prevention of deprivation in children'. Seven to nine experts believe that these aspects should be a part of education in child-care institutions, whereas the others didn't mention such goals. The answers have considerable overlap with answers given to another question 'What should be the function of a child-care centre?'

Functions of multicultural education in a child-care centre

Multicultural education in child-care centres can have several functions for children (majority and minority). The functions described by the experts often fall within three broad and somewhat overlapping categories:

(1) *Experience*: Multicultural education can offer children the opportunity to experience other cultures.
(2) *Knowledge*: Multicultural education can give children the opportunity to learn about different cultures.
(3) *Attitude*: Multicultural education may give children the opportunity to attach a positive value to their own and other cultures.

Offering multicultural *experiences* does not require an active policy in a child-care centre. A centre may have multicultural groups and thereby offer children multicultural experiences, but take no active role in doing something with these experiences. Creating opportunities for learning multicultural *knowledge* requires a more active role among child-care centres. A centre can remain relatively neutral and present knowledge without attaching any values. A centre is even more involved when it aims at influencing the way children *value* cultural experiences and knowledge. Nine experts believe this should be a function of multicultural education: encouraging a positive *attitude* towards the home culture (developing positive self-esteem), and other cultures (developing respect, tolerance and diversity for personal enrichment).

The question remains how far a child-care centre should go in their promotion of a multicultural society. Should it be a task for child-care centres to stimulate certain attitudes in children? A further interesting question is who should decide on this issue? Is it something that should be left to the caregivers and the centre, or should parents and society (for example local or national authorities) also be involved in this decision?

Multicultural education should have the same meaning for ethnic minority children and children from the majority culture, but for ethnic minority children it can have some additional functions. For such ethnic minority children multicultural education may encourage a positive attitude towards their own cultural background, stimulate the home language, and develop a positive self-image. Multicultural education may also facilitate the participation of immigrant children in the mainstream culture by learning about habits in the majority culture and learning the majority language. From these observations by experts, we obtained the impression that language stimulation in the majority and in the minority language should be an important part of multicultural education for ethnic minority children.

Besides its function for children, multicultural education can also have a value for parents. Some experts suggest that parents benefit when multicultural education is given to their children. Multicultural education in a child-care centre can offer something to children that is not offered at home, for example, the opportunity to relate to people from a variety of ethnic backgrounds and to learn more about other cultures. However, one can argue that this should only be seen as a positive function for parents if parents agree with the centre's multicultural policy.

Most of the experts see multicultural education as having a more direct function for the parents themselves: meeting people from other cultural backgrounds, and learning from each other. One participant pointed to the importance of developing solidarity by developing common interests between parents.

Multicultural education can have another specific function for immigrant parents. A multicultural child-care centre can give immigrant parents a place to find some recognition of their culture, accommodating their particular needs and acting as an institution where they are treated equally. Besides this, the centre can give immigrant parents support in their educator role, support against racism, and information and facilities for integration in the wider community.

The question remains whether a child-care centre should have a role focusing on the parents of the children and not on just the children themselves. Multicultural education in child-care centres can have meaning and value for the parents, but are centres really supposed to educate, support and inform parents beyond what would normally take place in parent–caregiver contacts? One can argue that often caregivers are not prepared to extend their role to include a parent focus.

According to the experts, society can benefit considerably from multicultural education. It can bring different cultures in society closer together, and can produce opportunities for social integration. In a child-care centre, children (and parents) learn about living in a multicultural context. This will enhance social understanding, and provide opportunities to learn how to operate in a culturally diverse society. In the long run, this may have a positive effect on society: (e.g. equal opportunities and treatment for all people regardless of culture, prevention of racism and other forms of discrimination). Society may also benefit from the optimisation of resources contained within ethnic minority groups.

We asked the experts to indicate which of the following goals for multicultural education they think are important. The numbers between the brackets refer to the number of experts choosing the goal.

(A)   Preparing children for their future lives in a multicultural society (15).
(B)   Adapting material and training staff to the presence of ethnic minority children (12).
(C)   Paying attention to different foods, hygiene and sleeping habits (12).
(D)   Paying attention to the development of ethnic minority children (8).
(E)   Paying special attention to developmental differences in ethnic minority children (5).
(F)   Paying special attention to the prevention of deprivation in ethnic minority children (7).
(G)   Paying special attention to the preparation of ethnic minority children for elementary schooling (7).
(H1) Encouraging the mother tongue in ethnic minority children (12).
(H2) Encouraging the majority language in ethnic minority children (12).
(I)   Giving children values and standards to increase acceptance of other cultures (13).
(J)   Give children knowledge on different cultures (12).
(K)   Encouraging playing/working with children from different ethnic backgrounds (14).
(L)   Making children familiar with adults from another ethnic background than their parents' (13).
(M)   Encouraging a positive self-image in ethnic minority children (14).

All experts agree that 'preparing children for their future lives in a multicultural society' is an important aspect of multicultural education in child-care institutions. Earlier on we showed that 'preparing children for their future lives in general' was mentioned by ten experts as an important goal for education in child-care centres. This suggests that multicultural education as a preparation for living in the multicultural society is conceived of as something quite distinct. Perhaps it is seen as a task that is not obvious to all responsible persons and institutions, or that it is a very difficult task and therefore deserves special attention.

Little prominence is given to aspects of multicultural education that are associated with special attention to the development of ethnic minority children (e.g. to screen for developmental differences, to prevent deprivation, to prepare for elementary schooling). The reason for this may relate to a preference 'not to stigmatise ethnic minority groups as deviant'.

Perhaps the use of the term 'special' attention functioned as a warning signal to most of the experts.

The encouragement of the mother tongue, the majority language and a positive self-image in ethnic minority children were seen as aspects important for multicultural education.

Discussion

The goals of that at least 13 of 18 experts (i.e. more than 66%) said are important for the general quality of ECCE institutions are as follows :

- Provide a familiar and stimulating environment for children.
- Encourage children's development.
- Provide a stimulating language environment.
- Give children knowledge about the world around them.
- Familiarise children with other children.
- Familiarise children with other adults.
- Encourage a positive self-image in children.

For most goals, the question remains how to enact them in working practice. We give two examples. The first goal (provide a familiar and stimulating environment) is rather simple. From studies, we know that continuity in adult caretakers and in peer relationships is important for young children to feel at ease and to engage in developmentally enriching activities (Howes & Hamilton, 1993; Raikes, 1993). Making the goal 'encourage children's development', more concrete is also difficult. Does the goal address social skills, communication skills, literacy, or motor skills some of these or all these? Experts were reluctant to give such precise detail. They appeared afraid of a departmentalisation of the curriculum, which would not be consistent with the notion of a holistic approach being best for young children. A holistic approach is characterised by ample opportunities for children to choose activities which they like most. The assumption is that children will choose what at a particular moment, is best suited to their development. Children are seen as self-initiators and self-regulators of their own development (Clarke-Stewart, 1991, 1993). A condition for this to occur is that they feel safe and secure and have enough of an overview of a situation to pick 'developing' opportunities. If children don't feel safe, or are not able to structure their environment, they cannot make sensible choices and the assumption becomes unrealistic. This developmental/educational concept has been skilfully depicted by Van Geert (1991, 1992b). In order for young children to be able to pick the appropriate developmental opportunities, a well structured curriculum can be of great help to them. Structured curricula do not necessarily restrict children's initiative and self-regulation. They give children a solid foundation, a recognition of activity patterns and opportunities for choice (cf. Leseman, 1994).

As to goals of multicultural education, experts agree on the importance of the following:

- Prepare children for their future lives in a multicultural society.
- Teach children values that stimulate acceptance of other cultures.
- Familiarise children with adults from different ethnic backgrounds.
- Encourage a positive self-image in ethnic minority children.

The experts are clearly in favour of multicultural education for all children. They mentioned only one specific goal: concerning ethnic minority children's self-image. This response is surprising because the experts had already agreed on the importance of the encouragement of children's self-image as a general goal . However, the experts clearly emphasised the importance of self-image among ethnic minority children. This preference suggests that there is something problematic about ethnic minority children's self-image, although studies don't confirm this (cf. Vedder, 1993). Other specific goals, whose relevance has been highlighted by research, for instance, concerning the prevention of learning problems, were not chosen by more than eight experts.

Stimulating children's language development was mentioned as a goal that is important for a centres' general quality. The specific focus on multilingual education, stressing the importance of children's first language, just failed to meet our criterion. Twelve of the 18 experts named this goal. This outcome indicates the controversial nature of this goal, even amongst experts. Beliefs such as 'children's mastery of their first language will facilitate learning the second language' are too simple and therefore, in many, situations misleading. Contextual variables such as parents' and children's language attitudes, language practices at home, standardisation of the first languages, availability of language assistants and programmes, all should be considered when deciding whether stimulating children's first language proficiency is an option which benefits all children. In the Netherlands, an increasing number of immigrant parents, themselves born and raised in the Netherlands, make a choice to speak Dutch to their children. It seems that the discussions on the importance of children's first language in institutional education is being overtaken by language shift towards the majority language in immigrant groups (cf. Vedder, Muysken & Kook, in prep.; Kook & Vedder, 1994). A simple belief in the first language maintenance rule may be valuable, but only in particular settings (cf. Cummins, 1990; Siguan, 1990).

The experts agree that stimulating children's social development and the development of play are important functions for child-care centres. Other development domains, such as cognitive, artistic and physical development, are deemed less important. The experts seem rather reluctant to specify goals for child-care centres at the level of children's development. They prefer to define goals in terms of the creation of enriching environments. For instance, they stress the importance of providing a familiar and stimulating environment for children. Another more specific example is the creation of a stimulating language environment with attention to children's mother tongue as well as to the language of the wider community. A corresponding goal in children's development (stimulating children's language proficiency) is not seen as an important goal.

We also found unanimity among the experts in rejecting children's preparation for elementary school as a function for child-care centres. Attention to the prevention of learning problems, the detection of developmental problems and focusing on academic skills is seen as less desirable than other centre goals. Such attention may contribute to stigmatisation of ethnic minority groups. However, most experts think that child-care centres can have a function in preventing learning problems in ethnic minority children. How this is or should be accomplished, is unclear.

Although experts are reluctant to define the value of child-care centres in terms of a contribution to children's future functioning in school and society, they agree on the importance of preparing children for their future lives in a multicultural society. Appreciation of cultural diversity is seen as an important attitudinal goal.

Child-care centres also have functions for parents and for society. They allow parents to go out for work or engage in other activities, they give parents opportunities to share educational experiences and to seek educational advice. A multicultural centre can give parents opportunities to meet persons from a variety of cultural backgrounds and to learn about these cultures. Parents, moreover, may find support against prejudice and discrimination, and obtain information and facilities for integration into the wider community.

The societal functions of child-care centres are also seen to include women's emancipation and the development of a new distribution of educational responsibilities in which a society may locate new ways for assuming its responsibility for young children's socialisation.

Most experts were in favour of looking at multicultural education as a quality criterion of effectiveness in all centres.

Conclusion

Our presentation of the goal preferences among three parties involved in determining what goals are important for ECCE and multicultural education in ECCE, clarified that, in each party, we could identify majorities agreeing on the importance of particular goals. At the same time, however, we have located disagreements about other goals, both within and between parties. For instance, with regard to the preparation for primary school and the social goals of respect for adults and obedience, many immigrant parents disagree with the majority of Dutch parents, but also with centre staff. Centre staff and Dutch parents agree that centres do not have a role in preparing children for school and that children's social development is very important. Stressing social development, however, centre staff and Dutch parents refer to peer relationships, whereas immigrant parents' primary concern is adult–child relationships. Most experts deem attention to children's mother tongue important, but centre staff do not share the same enthusiasm or prioritisation.

At a general level, one can define goals that majorities in all parties agree on. The goal 'Provide a safe and secure environment for children' is an important focus, but what constitutes such an environment? Would all children feel safe and secure in the same type of environment? It simply is a goal which is not very clear or tangible and its achievement is hard to realise by training or policy measures.

A goal such as 'encouraging children's development' is also far too general. One group might want more attention to children's cognitive development, whereas another group may want to encourage children's language or social development.

The conclusion has to be that it is very difficult to find an exact, explicit or tacit consensus about goals for ECCE in general or for multicultural education, that are so clear and concrete that they can be used to evaluate the quality of ECCE and multicultural education in ECCE. Parents' and teachers' cultural backgrounds, their knowledge about the educational system and about child development, their capability of assessing what is good for their children's development, parents and staffs' mutual dependency and many other factors combine to influence goal preferences. Can social scientists help?

The Social Scientists' Role

In Chapter 1, we stated (and in this chapter we clarified) that knowing what goals are important in ECCE and multicultural education ideally require explicit or tacit consensus between educators. Social scientists working in this field rarely consider this problem (see, however, Moss, 1988). They either assume a consensus exists or they anticipate a consensus about a particular goal. For instance, they assume that an intelligence test is a good measure for the goal 'prepare children for the cognitive requirements of primary school'. Their research informs us about the means that are effective regarding this goal. A list as in Table 6.1 may be the result. It is an adapted version of a list produced by White (1985). The variables in White's list are distal variables that may facilitate the quality of care with respect to the goal to prepare children for the cognitive requirements of primary school, but such variables do not refer directly to educators and children's activities or experiences. Melhuish (1993) has presented a list of more proximal variables. We present this list in Table 6.2.

Although the variables in Melhuish's (1993) list reflect more educational practices, it is still not an agenda for an educational programme. A programme requires clear choices. This is particularly evident in the variable 'developmentally appropriate activities' which are still not suffi-ciently defined. Clarke-Stewart (1991) suggests that these might be programmes with more prescribed educational activities such as lessons, guided play sessions and the teaching of specific content. Using such a programme leads to higher scores on intelligence and achievement tests, but might restrict children's opportunities for peer interaction, meaning that children may have fewer opportunities to develop social skills. These and comparable lists (see e.g. Riksen-Walraven, 1992), clearly have

Table 6.1 Most frequently reported development enhancing variables in studies on the effects of early childhood programmes (assumed goal: prepare children for the cognitive requirements of primary school)

Variable	Most Frequent Conclusions
Parental involvement	More is better
Age intervention begins	Earlier is better
Duration/intensity	Longer/more intense is better
Degree of structure	More structure is better
Training of interveners	More is better
Continuity with public school	Enhances intervention
Type of curriculum	No one type is better
Individualization	More is better
Child/caregiver ratio	Lower is better

Table 6.2 Proximal variables indicating the quality of education in child-care centres

Variable	Specification
Adult–child interaction:	Sensitive responsiveness, communication, emotional security
Peer interaction:	More interaction — social skills improve
Interpersonal relationships:	Attachment, stability of relationships
Developmentally appropriate activities:	Most appropriate situations defined by zone of proximal development
Health and safety:	A.o. disease control
Emotional climate 'happiness':	Active, happy, involved children — happiness makes learning easier

shortcomings: they assume consensus about goals and they lack clues as to what choices should be made in a curriculum.

Social scientists can have an important function in the elucidation of such goals. The process of goal formulation and consensus reaching depends on knowledge about what are feasible goals and what are the means to achieve such goals. Scientists clearly can contribute to this knowledge and inform practising educators about it. In this way, social scientists can contribute to the development of good quality care.

An example may be found in the work of Dickinson and Snow and their colleagues. They explored what role preschools play in stimulating children's vocabulary and discourse skills (Dickinson, 1993; Snow, 1993). They found that children profit most from small group discussions and round table conversations about topics that require that children are explicit about a context. They have to contextualise information for the other children to be understood. Decontextualised language skills can be developed, for instance, through extended talk, explaining things and transmitting knowledge about a 'not immediately visible' world. Pretend play is another activity stimulating these rich kinds of interactions. The use of decontextualised language skills appears to be a good predictor of children's literacy development. Story reading and telling also may be enriching to the extent that children themselves get involved in extended talk, in analysing the story and giving explanations for things that happen or might have happened. Indeed children's involvement and activities are important for their development, but caregivers play an irreplaceable role in giving them stimuli, asking them questions, encouraging them to stop and talk and think about what they are doing, and supporting them to find ways to richer communication.

This chapter now continues by clarifying a social scientists' role more extensively with regard to two issues in multicultural education: learning problems and multilingual education.

Learning problems

Many child-care centres in the Netherlands and abroad don't have a clear stated responsibility in preparing children for school (see Chapters 3 and 4). Yet, social scientists stress the possible role of child-care centres delivering such preparation.

In this section, we describe two possible ways in which caregivers may deal with developmental and learning problems in child-care centres: (1) there is a need for special attention to such problems, but the type and content of such attention are independent of the children's cultural ethnic background; (2) such special attention is required and it should be geared to the specific needs of children; these needs vary between ethnic cultural groups.

Special attention irrespective of children's ethnic-cultural background

This approach recently is strongly supported in the Netherlands by research which suggests that learning problems in schoolchildren can be explained by indices for socioeconomic status irrespective of children's cultural-ethnic background (Commissie Allochtone Leerlingen in het Onderwijs, 1992). The extra attention is given through general measures to improve the learning environment. This approach is also well known in the USA (Slavin, Karweit & Madden, 1989; who also detail effective measures). However, not only is the approach's effectiveness decisive for its supporters. For many of them, another important rationale is that attention geared to the particular needs of children from a variety of cultural ethnic groups, or approaches in which differences between groups are stressed, might contribute to children's isolation and even to ethnic conflict, prejudice and discrimination (Stone, 1981; Vedder, 1993).

Special attention taking children's background into account

This approach is represented in Model 2 (facilitation of a shift between home culture and mainstream culture) and an important premise is that, for children's well-being, child-care centres should try to adapt their care and education to children's care and education at home. A gap between home and centre education is seen as a risk factor in developmental problems. Working with children from a variety of cultural backgrounds means that closing this gap requires staff flexibility in cultural adaptation strategies. Different children expect different forms of attention dependent on their particular family background (Ogbu, 1992; Pels, 1993).

Attention to bridging the gap between centre and home, or between school and home, may be more than just a preventive measure. Moll (1992) shows that it may be very stimulating for children's learning to use knowledge and skill resources that are readily available in their own, or their families' social network, and this may contribute to overcoming developmental and learning problems.

This approach, however, may take on dubious forms if it is inspired by an extreme notion of cultural relativism of learning and learning problems. In this view what is deemed normal for one cultural group (e.g. the Moroccan), is different from what is deemed normal for another group (e.g. the Dutch). Consequently, what is deemed abnormal, or problematic is also conceived of as different. From this standpoint one might hear a statement like: 'Why bother about a lack of autonomy, initiative and creativity in Moroccan children. Their parents don't appreciate it. They see autonomy, initiative and creativity as abnormal' (cf. Swieringa, 1986). The consequence of such a notion is that Moroccan children in a Western child-care centre are evaluated, as a group, with different standards than other children. This notion denies that cultural values for development and education a) are not equally appreciated by all individual members of a culture; b) are changeable and negotiable with persons and institutions important and responsible for a child's development and learning. Moreover, c) it denies that immigrant children no longer live in a country far away, but in the Netherlands. They need to learn to cope with their Dutch environment.

Multilingual education

Multilingual education refers to educators' attempts to stimulate children's language proficiency in more than one language and to learn to make correct language choices that accord with the communication setting.

Multilingual education is related to learning problems. A high percentage of immigrant children in the Netherlands lack in Dutch language proficiency (Extra & Verhoeven, 1993). Multilingual education is seen as a means to avoid the insufficient language competence turning into learning problems. Multilingual education is a special educational approach taking children's language background into account.

Apart from a prevention function, multilingual education in child-care centres may have other functions. It can be a means to stress the importance and status of children's mother tongue. This may encourage children and parents to maintain verbal interaction in the only language that many parents really master, their mother tongue. This may be accomplished by allowing or encouraging children to use their mother tongue in the centre, or by showing a positive attitude towards variety in mother tongues. Using children's mother tongue can also be a means to smooth the transfer from home to centre and contribute to children's social and emotional well-being.

Apart from using children's mother tongue, attention to multilingual education also affects the caregivers' attitudes. And attention to Dutch as a second or third language is part of a multilingual education policy.

No single best approach for young children

Models for multilingual education mainly address two questions: (1) What is the role of the centre and the parents and (2) Should children learn two or more languages simultaneously or successively (Veen & Vermeulen, 1993)? Combining the answers to these questions results in four descriptive models of language practices presented in Figure 6.1.

That parents also encourage their young children to understand and speak the second language is very real, but is not represented in the figure. Here we pay more attention to a centre's approach and the situation that children don't speak Dutch at home.

Whether two languages should be learned successively or simultaneously is a question that lacks a clear-cut answer. The fear is that simultaneous contacts with two languages may confuse children, which may lead to some retardation of children's language development (Snow, 1992). Whether it has some negative consequences, however, depends on the way the contacts between the languages are organised and on how

Figure 6.1 Practices of multilingual education as a responsibility of child-care centres and parents

	Simultaneous	Successive
Centre	Stimulates first and second language	Stimulates first language and after a period the second language
Parents	Stimulate first language	Stimulate first language
Centre	Stimulates second language	Stimulates second language
Parents	Stimulate first language	Stimulate first language

encouraging and enriching children's experiences are (Cummins, 1990). Other important factors are parents' attitudes towards the languages, their language skills and language contacts, and the centre's language approach (Veen & Vermeulen, 1993). The fear of language problems resulting from simultaneous attention to two or more languages leads to the option of a successive approach, which normally means that a centre will try to communicate with the children, at least the very young, in their mother tongue.

A simultaneous approach is likely to have benefits. Mastering a language at a level that allows for effective use in academic settings takes a long time. Not starting second language acquisition early means that children are not often sufficiently proficient in their second language when they start primary school. This leads to problems if the second language is the language of instruction. Thus it seems that the best child-care centres can do is to encourage children to use Dutch as a second language right from the start. Moreover, the general notion seems that young children are more successful in learning a second language than older children and adults. They are less frustrated when making errors as a result of experimenting with language production. Moreover, starting young gives a better guarantee that children succeed in using the second language in a native like fashion (B. McLaughlin, 1987).

Scientific evidence that attention to children's first language reduces the likelihood of mastering a second language is not conclusive. Experiments and demonstration projects show that approaches fostering a simultaneous attention to a variety of languages can be beneficial for learning a second language (Cziko, 1992). A more serious argument against using immigrant children's first language is the shortage of qualified educators who speak children's first language.

Conclusion

In this chapter, we have attempted to answer the question 'What should multicultural education in ECCE look like', or formulated differently 'What is good quality ECCE and multicultural education in ECCE?' We could not find a generally applicable measure for good quality ECCE and multicultural education. Such a measure depends on a consensus about goals between the educators and institutions responsible for ECCE and multicultural education. In the Netherlands, parents and centre staff have the primary responsibility. National and community administration and centre boards take responsibility for housing, hygiene, safety and staff qualifications. Staff and parents of particular centres should reach a consensus about important goals as a prerequisite for assessing quality in their centre.

Social scientists can aid the processes of goal formulation and consensus building, in that they can show whether means are available and practicable whether it is possible to realistically achieve particular goals. Social science researchers are valuable when goals have been set. We highlighted this when dealing with two issues in multicultural education: learning problems and multilingual education.

As to the social scientists' role, however, an important conclusion is that social scientists cannot change an earlier conclusion that good quality education is a relative concept depending on the values of different individuals and groups. Researchers can only define this concept if, apart from what they already do, they find ways to grasp and represent the dynamic process of consensus building about educational goals.

7 Consensus Building

Our search for important goals for ECCE and multicultural education in ECCE has led us to a conclusion that generally applicable goals are either so abstract that they are not practicable, or they do not exist in large, culturally diverse groups, because a broad consensus on goals between all those responsible for ECCE and multicultural education, irrespective of particular groups, is not feasible. Nevertheless, the quality of ECCE and multicultural education in ECCE can neither be assessed, nor improved unless we know what goals are important. If we cannot find generally applicable goals, an alternative might be to look for locally applicable goals based on a consensus between persons responsible for the education in just one centre or a few local centres. In this chapter, we introduce a strategic model, the consensus model, which gives guidelines as to how educators can work towards a consensus. The notion of responsiveness plays an important role in this model.

Responsivity: A Prerequisite for Quality in ECCE and Multicultural Education

As previously stated, the quality of ECCE in general and the quality of multicultural education are mutually interdependent. If a centre operates below generally accepted standards, we cannot expect it to meet specific needs. On the other hand, education in a multi-ethnic setting requires the evaluation of existing quality standards and might eventually lead to a better formulation of existing standards or to the development of new standards.

According to developmental theories inspired by Vygotsky (Van Geert, 1992a; Wertsch, 1979), development maximally occurs when educators adapt their regulatory and instructive behaviour to the 'zone of proximal development'. A key condition is the ability to sense what the child can understand, to interpret the child's signals, and a willingness to react accordingly, in other words, to show sensitive responsiveness.

As we argued previously, developmental and educational goals may differ considerably between cultures. This means that zones of proximal

100

development are not culturally free either. Educators may respond sensitively to widely different behaviours and by doing so, they stimulate their children in different domains of development. Whether the physical stimulation of babies is the focus, the play with infants, or the socialisation of 4-year-olds, large cultural differences occur. For instance, the inter-actions of mothers with their babies in Mali, Senegal or Morocco are mostly geared to orienting them to their social environment (by smacking lips, naming and adapting their posture) and less to manipulation and exploration of objects as occurs in Western families. Infants are quick in learning concepts expressing varying sorts of family relationships and behaviour suitable in different social circumstances. Children thus stimu-lated show considerable social skills early in life (Pels, 1991; Rabain-Jamain, 1989). Within migrant families, the amount of object-oriented interaction and how it develops, is framed within their cultural-specific social environment.

Sensitivity and responsiveness to such cultural differences mean that caregivers help children in using already acquired skills and knowledge as resources for further learning. One goal hence becomes the facilitation of children's transition between home and centre. This, however, is only achieved if the sensitivity and responsiveness is linked to a clear under-standing of what knowledge and skills should be learned by children to be able to succeed with tasks that are set for them in the centre, at home and in other environments. Moreover, caregivers' responsivity should lead to activities that give children a feeling of security, belonging and mastery. It is valuable for caregivers and other professional educators to recognise that particular homes provide children with particular socialisation contexts which prepare them differentially for tasks in the centre than other homes. A lack of such knowledge may lead to some educators 'blaming the victim'. Instead, such educators need to understand and accommodate the cultural variations between homes, and between such homes and the school. Such an understanding includes an awareness of the differing educational goals among different cultures.

A change towards more sensitivity and responsiveness ideally means a willingness to adapt to cultural differences. Such cultural adaptation ideally leads to changes in interactional style and choice of activities.

Apart from knowledge and skill domains, educational responsiveness has another function for young children that is at least as important, viz. expressing a positive attitude towards cultural differences. This function comes very close to the most general goal of multicultural education in child-care centres: mutual accommodation and respect between people from different cultural-ethnic backgrounds. For various reasons, the practicality of implementing this ideal is limited.

To begin with, power relations within society exercise a strong influence on the development of cultural models (Foucault, 1980). Thus, when processes of acculturation take place, more often than not, changes are in the direction of the dominant culture. Another constraint resides in psychological factors. Every adult is 'culturally relative', feeling safe within his or her native culture. Opening up to values that are radically different can cause feelings of threat and result in resistance (Smeyers, 1991). This is true for caregivers in child-care centres and possibly even more for parents from ethnic groups in a subordinated societal position. Another constraint in the process of mutual adaptation resides in the challenged cultural elements. Acculturation is often a lengthy process. The more fundamental the values at stake, the more they are potentially mutually conflicting (Eldering, 1993). The development of individual autonomy, for instance, is a fundamental Western value that will rarely be negotiable within child care education settings.

However, the fact that centres try to stimulate children's autonomy or independence and openness to explore their environment and communicate with peers and adults alike is probably not a problem to the children themselves. They still are in the process of enculturation: they have not yet acquired a set of fixed habits. Their world view is diffuse and they are oriented towards others rather than to their 'enculturated' individual selves (Aboud, 1987). They have a high tolerance of cultural discontinuity. Presumably, because of their strong attachment and orientation to significant others in their environment, small children are only troubled by negative reactions to cultural differences of those significant others (Secord & Backman, 1974).

Therefore, we should regard the value attached by parents and caregivers to (elements of) their culture, and consequently, the way they react to differences, of the utmost importance. Ethnocentric or negative attitudes from caregivers to children's cultural and language background cannot co-exist with what is most central to quality education: sensitive responsiveness. Such attitudes are detrimental to adult–child and peer interactions. Likewise, negative attitudes of parents to educational settings outside the home can prevent children from being actively and happily involved, and from establishing open relationships (e.g. Pels, 1991).

The meaning and affect attached to elements of family culture can differ between members of ethnic groups and between specific situations. For instance, if parents value obedience and respect in their children at home, they can nevertheless encourage them to adapt to the cultural ethos of individuality in non-maternal educational settings. Their motivation for mobility might encourage parents to stimulate 'biculturality' in their children (Kagitçibasi, 1987, 1989; Pels, 1991). In contrast, ambivalence towards mobility through education can lead parents to stress the threat of mainstream educational institutions to their culture (see for example Ogbu, 1992; Vermeulen, 1992). This clarifies that responsiveness is not just important for the relationship between caregivers and children, but also between caregivers and children's other educators.

What has been said thus far leads us to the following conclusions. When considering goals in multicultural education, the dynamic and creative character of culture should be considered, as well as the specific needs, possibilities and perceptions of small children, their parents and caregivers. Especially with regard to young children, parents and centre staff's positive attitudes towards cultural differences are more crucial to their well-being than the bridging of cultural differences, achieved by teaching children particular skills and knowledge.

Responsiveness towards children's developmental needs is best accomplished when parents and professional caregivers cooperate with mutual respect. In being responsive towards parents, caregivers in essence have to meet the same criteria that are relevant to a sensitive support of children. Riksen-Walraven (1992) lists four tasks important for professionals when they are supporting parents:

- to give information and explanation;
- to offer structure;
- to respond sensitively to parent's needs and perceptions;
- to respect parent's autonomy and competence as educators.

Not all caregivers will be equally competent in fulfilling these tasks. Many will need guidance and further training.

A policy of responsiveness means that children's culture linked knowledge and skill resources are explored and used to further their development. Responsivity to parents means that one respects their educational values. In an educational setting, however, this does not necessarily lead to attempts to inculcate these values in the children. Responsivity to other parents, to colleagues and to children may lead to an educational values agenda that is quite distinct from the agenda of individual parents. Notions on responsivity will have to be further specified in terms of strategies of responsivity to parents and children, how to teach and learn these, how to combine responsivity with educational tasks and goals that are deemed important for all children, and how to find a balanced values agenda and activities programme in which all caregivers, parents and children feel respected. Some of these specifications are discussed in the next model: the consensus model.

The Consensus Model

The consensus model is primarily concerned with caregivers, parents and other groups that are, or want themselves to be, responsible for children's education. At the heart of the model is the notion of preschool's relative autonomy.

Relative autonomy

The notion of relative autonomy stems from the 'Geisteswissen-schaftliche' and Marxist traditions in pedagogy, that mainly flourished between 1920 and 1980 in Germany (Beutler, 1969; Bohnsack & Rückriem, 1969; Heydorn, 1970; Huisken, 1974; Klafki, 1963; Nohl, 1967; Schiess, 1973). Representatives of these traditions were concerned about the influence of political interest groups in education. They conceived of interest groups as pressure groups trying to control education by using their power to implement a curriculum that met their interests. To limit the influence of these external forces, educators examined possibilities of sheltering educational institutions from these forces. In practice, this sometimes led to an extreme selection of curricular content, making educational institutions places for learning and development that lacked functionality outside the institution.

In the Netherlands, although not clearly inspired by pedagogical traditions as mentioned above, this focus on curricular selection to generate the relative autonomy of preschools is particularly clear from negative evaluations of proposals to introduce a curriculum in preschools that more directly prepares children for an effective transition into primary schools (see Chapter 3). In democracies, educational institutions can have a relative degree of autonomy, as a right or through a fight. They do not have to be directly responsive to any demand for change. Proposals for curricular change are filtered through available resources such as caregivers attitudes and knowledge, support by parents and others, children's capacities and financial arrangements. Interest groups not directly involved in education cannot simply influence a pedagogical climate in an institution (Coleman & Collinge, 1991; M. McLaughlin, 1987).

An institution's relative autonomy may operate in several ways. It may be used to continue the use of the inherited curriculum that has been in use for many years, or it may be used as a position from which professional educators can coordinate and work towards a policy of responsiveness, towards a movement for change.

Explicit and tacit consensus

A policy of responsiveness may take shape from a discussion between a variety of groups or forces that have (or claim) a say in the organisation and curriculum of child-care centres. Children, parents, caregivers, boards, representatives of business groups and local and national administrators might be important groups in this discussion (Singer, 1992; Vedder, 1992). Ideally the discussion between these participants should result in explicit consensus about the goals that should be attained in the centre, on how each person can contribute to achieve the centre's goals and about whom is accountable to whom for what aspects of care and education that contribute to, or hamper, the attainment of the goals.

Such discussions rarely take place. The discussion normally doesn't occur in a meeting with all participants present and within a preplanned period. It is often more a process of chained incidents or conflicts. For instance, representatives of companies may negotiate with national or local administrators for guaranteed places in child-care centres. The companies pay for the places, but formulate, as a condition, their desire for high quality centres. The administrators and companies agree to install a committee that will offer advice about the quality of child-care centres. The negotiations and conclusions are reported by the news media. This motivates other institutions to react and to claim a place on the central committee or to reject the committee's advice and formulate their own quality requirements. Often this process ends in the acceptance of a situation of negative coordination (Lundgren, 1983). This is a situation in which different interest groups, each stressing different aims and functions of education, evaluate that, under given circumstances, their interests are being met in a satisfactory manner. They no longer discuss similarities and differences or wish to reach a tacit consensus. This may subsequently result in the situation as Bruner (1980) described for England's under fives. He depicted preschool curricula as a potpourri of activities to satisfy the varied interests of many groups.

Educational values have to be communicated or negotiated. Although some values may be very personal and difficult to communicate, there is reason to believe that it is feasible to develop a notion of shared values. People residing in a community try to make themselves predictable to each other so as to achieve a certain stability in their relationships and to a sense of belonging. They are willing to reach consensus and stick to it, because this is a precondition for stability and is integral to a rewarding sense of belonging. Van de Graaf and Hoppe (1989) describe this position as the 'ethics of good reason', in which discourse, dialectic exchange between value positions, and persuasion to establish the acceptability of policies are emphasised. The ethics of good reason seems a feasible concept, but it certainly doesn't lead to a consensus that stands definitively or statically.

Taylor (1991) suggests that the process of development towards a consensus is important and not the product. One of the reasons is that consensus is not a stable quality. Participants in the discussion may change, and those who stay may develop or change their ideas and preferences. Values that were part of the consensus can be amended and will evolve. Taylor suggests that the more attention to the products of consensus reaching (for instance written charters or codes of conduct), the less chance there is to respond to changes in values, and the more chance that consensus seeking will lead to conflicts.

In contemporary society, is it hard to imagine that all citizens will reach a complete consensus about a large set of values that will guide educational practices in all preschools. Yet, living in conflict is not necessarily the alternative. We have discussed preschools' relative autonomy. Relative autonomy means that preschool staff have the opportunity to adapt curricula to the values and needs of a smaller community within a society. Ideas about important values in a wider community may be coordinated with more local values or needs. This makes the notion of relative autonomy an instrument for conflict management when working with the consensus model.

Mechanisms for reaching consensus

Consensus can be reached either by selection, by consensus building through discussions, or by a combination of selection and consensus building.

Selection occurs when a centre informs parents about their goals and processes and discourages or forbids parents who do not agree with these goals and processes in bringing their children to the centre. A less rigorous means of selection is self selection, meaning that parents themselves decide that a particular centre is not what they desire for their children. A prerequisite of this model is that a centre has a clear notion of goals and means that can be presented in a way that allows parents to understand them and compare them to a notion of own preferences. For self-selection this is enough, but for a pro-active form of selection, centre staff have to investigate parents' preferred educational goals and processes. This is an almost impossible task for a centre, because many parents either have no well defined notion of educational goals and processes, or they can't or don't feel like informing centre staff about them. This will be the case if parents realise that the information they give might be used to deny their child a place, which is a far from rewarding prospect.

One can conceive of mono-ethnic centres in a multicultural neighbourhood (like Centre H; see Chapter 4) as the result of consensus achieved through selection and self-selection.

Consensus building is the process of clarifying one's own notions about educational goals and processes in discussions with other people (staff and other parents) to compare these notions and to argue why particular goals and processes are better than others. Convincing partners in the discussion is an important ingredient of consensus building. Since discussion may change partners' ideas about effective goals and means, the consensus building process is ideally a continuing process. Although deciding about the goals and means that are agreeable to all participants and writing them down may be important to give a sense of stability to the process, these products eventually are less important than the process. This dynamic character implies that not reaching a consensus on all goals or means is not fatal for the consensus. One has to try to reach a consensus on a subset of the broad variety of goals and means that are under discussion. This core set unites the persons involved in the discussion and gives clarity about the aims and mission of the centre. The points of disagreement provide a stimulus for further discussion.

Parent committees, home–centre contact facilitators, the organisation of conversation groups in parents' first language, the availability of first language speaking staff, and many other initiatives that were mentioned in preceding chapters to facilitate parent involvement, may be helpful in establishing consensus building practices.

It should be clear that staff play an important role in these practices. They are the facilitators, the primary responsible organisers. They are not simply the ones who eventually will have to enact parents preferences. They can inform parents about the feasibility of particular goals and means, and they can try to convince parents that particular goals and means are important whereas others are not. Staff have to check whether parents will comply to a centre's rules and exercise their responsibilities as educators in supporting the care and education in the centre. Moreover, they have to inform new parents about the consensus and the ongoing consensus building process. Since both parents and their children are transitory, the staff provide the best guarantee of the continuity of the consensus building process.

A period of consensus building might be followed by attempts to maintain a consensus through selection or self-selection. Although this may be justified for a limited period in order to have enough stability to evaluate whether the consensus about goals and means is operating successfully, selection strategies should never be used for more than two years in nurseries and one year in playgroups. In these periods, half of the parents change, which means that the continuation of the consensus building process is jeopardised, because the new parents have not been involved.

If functioning well, a consensus building process is a valuable source of in-service training for staff, and provides a course in education and care for the parents. To facilitate this, parents and staff may decide occasionally to invite an expert to give a lecture or they might try to cooperate with an expert who is willing to function as an information source on a more regular basis. The expert, however, should not be seen as the one who definitively knows what is best. A good curriculum or activity plan will only result from clear notions about goals and means, and a knowledge of the personal (the children, the caregivers and parents) and material conditions (materials, classrooms, etc.) under which a curriculum plan has to be implemented. Experts can provide information on the feasibility of goals and the general quality of means in relation to the goals. However, the caregivers and parents often know most about material and personal conditions.

Conditions for consensus building

First, consensus building cannot operate without an anti-discrimination policy, guaranteeing (for all parents, children and staff) respect and acceptance in the centre and suitable measures if their sense of security is jeopardised. Parents and staff will be willing to invest in consensus building efforts only if they feel safe. A second important condition is responsivity in caregivers; responsivity towards parents and children. Responsivity is the skill and art of interacting with people in a way that assures others that it is rewarding to invest in a process of further learning and development in which persons work together, supporting each other. A third condition is parent involvement, or family involvement. This latter term (family involvement) is probably preferable, since it takes into account that not all children's primary educators are their parents. We shall now take a closer look at this condition.

Parent involvement

With the relative lack of interest in preschool education by many sections of the population and many institutions in most European countries (see

Moss, 1988), centre staff and parents are the most important participants in the consensus building process. This restriction of the range of persons and groups involved in the discussion seems to make the implementation of the consensus model a relatively simple task. In practice, however, parent involvement can provide difficulties.

Through their attention to children's behaviour in the centre, their involvement in preschool activities and their attitude, parents affect children's achievements, attitudes and aspirations (Coleman & Collinge, 1991). Caregivers and most parents know this (Payne & Hinds, 1986), and yet they don't easily locate ways to use this knowledge productively. Such parties may even find themselves in conflict with each other. This happens, for instance, when parents start complaining about the quality of education in terms of what they think is best for their individual child, whereas the caregiver has to look after the well-being of a whole group of children. Another source of conflict is the attitude of caregivers who emphasise that, while children are in the centre, parents should leave all educational responsibilities to the professional educator. Not only are parents being excluded from what is primarily their educational task, but they also get the message that, for the good of the child, they may best leave education to a professional (cf. Singer, 1992).

Caregivers create a professional autonomy, which at first may give them a feeling of empowerment, but eventually conflicts with their professional task and undermines their position. The caregivers' task is to provide an educational context that meets both children's interests and those of the communities they live in. Studies show that to achieve this, caregivers and parents should develop greater understanding and respect for the role each plays in the education of the child (Coleman & Collinge, 1991).

When staff grant parents a voice in deciding the goals and activities of centre care and education, they should not tacitly assume that they and the parents hold the same ideas about important goals and means. We have already shown that, even within centres, staff members do not always agree about goals and means, and we know from studies (Eldering & Vedder, 1992; Jap-a-Joe & Leseman, 1994; Pels, 1991; Van der Leij, 1991; Vedder, 1995) that preferred goals and means vary considerably between, as well as within, immigrant groups. Moreover, parents' and caregivers' value preferences change, and their preferences for educational goals and means change according to changes in society and caregivers' and parents' position in society (Harkness & Super, 1993; Vedder, 1994).

Western child-care centres tend to stress children's emotional well-being and their cognitive, social and language development. However, the 'hidden' curriculum may transmit a far wider set of cultural meanings. As Hofstede has indicated (1989; 1991) yet child-care centres are rooted in a cultural model that favours individualism more than collectivism, egalitarianism more than authoritarianism, and rationalism more than moralism. What happens in child-care centres, why and how, is rarely made explicit, child-care centres transmit a concept of childhood interwoven with those values: (especially through the way caregivers interact with children, through stories told and even through the interior design). The importance of the uniqueness of the child, of individual development and of being able to explore and initiate, is rarely contested (Van Ballegooijen, 1984).

Elsewhere, however, more weight is given to behaviours on the opposite poles of the cultural dimensions just mentioned. For example, in Chinese early childhood education, good habits, self control, and appropriate behaviours are favoured (Lee, 1992). Research among Moroccan and Turkish families in the Netherlands indicates that the stimulation of behaviour according to moral and social standards (obedience, respect), rather than individual autonomy, is highly valued. Also such parents are oriented to pre-academic learning more than to the psychological development of their small children (Pels, 1991; Van der Leij, 1991).

To summarise: often staff's notions of important goals and means differ from those of parents. At the same time, we saw in Chapter 3 that centre staff wish to bridge the gap between home culture and centre culture. Parent involvement and parent participation are a means to accomplish this. In practice, however, parents rarely have a say in educational matters in the centre. Staff may listen carefully to parents wishes as to particular care patterns and food preferences, but little more. For the good of the children, this should change. Continuity in educational goals and means between home and centre, or at least mutual support between home and centre, is bound to improve the achievement of important goals, which, by definition and in practice, would benefit the quality of children's education (Coleman & Collinge, 1991; Stevenson, 1992).

Often, what will emanate from a consensus between staff and parents is a set of goals and means that are more or less typical of one or more of the earlier presented descriptive models of multicultural education.

Experts' Evaluation of the Consensus Model

We invited 18 experts, ten Dutch and eight from other West European countries to a workshop to discuss the consensus model. They are the same experts who participated in the study presented in the preceding chapter (see also Appendix 1).

Some experts suggested that the consensus model is too naive in that power differences in society are insufficiently taken into account. They pointed out, that although communication between parents and professionals is of the utmost importance, staff cannot, and actually don't, decide amongst themselves about the quality of ECCE and multicultural education. Through materials, financing, housing contracts, and other important elements in the organisation of ECCE, other organisations affect what happens (and does not happen) in centres.

We used the notion of relative autonomy to underline the feasibility of the consensus model. Indeed, as suggested, the relative autonomy idea guarantees a shelter for a collaborative effort of parents and professionals to improve the quality of ECCE and multicultural education, but the adjective 'relative' indicates that other institutions in society still affect what is happening.

A few experts stated that the consensus model leads to lengthy discussions and that we cannot wait for discussions about a consensus that never will be reached. 'Open a centre with minority staff and minority children, adapt your fees to parental income and adapt your opening hours. Start right away and don't discuss it. When you start a discussion, you will end up with a lot of "yes, but...", and then it will never start.'

Most experts, however, didn't agree with this statement. They tried to define conditions for the model's implementation. The need for this was indicated by the fact that many parents are glad they find a place for their children, because it allows them to work. They have no interest in active involvement as is proposed by the consensus model. Moreover, many parents, particularly minority parents, see the caregiver primarily as a professional and not as a co-educator. Some rarely talk to a caregiver, and certainly would not say anything that could be taken as a directive.

The issue then becomes how can centres work with parents and enable parents to express their needs. Centres first have to create in parents a feeling of autonomy and security. A first step might be to show parents that the door is always open, that they are welcome to come in and to stay for a while to drink a cup of coffee, to watch the children, or just to chat. Staff can then sit with them and listen to them. From there on, staff can try and create some structure, for instance by suggesting that it would be nice if the parents come inside the centre every day when bringing their child. After such a preparation phase, caregivers might begin asking for information from the parents. What are changes that parents experienced since the child attended a centre? Are there any changes in the use of language in the family, and how do the children and parents feel about that? Regarding specific tasks (sleeping, eating, but also first and second language learning) caregivers might ask what things are particularly important for the parents. A next step might be for staff to agree to the following rule: In case you don't know what to do with a child, don't start guessing, but ask the parents what is the matter and what to do about it.

Implementing such rules should help in orienting towards parents' and children's educational wishes and needs.

Conclusion

So far the concept of consensus has been presented as the key to answering the questions 'What should ECCE and multicultural education in ECCE look like?' and 'How to improve ECCE and multicultural education in ECCE?'

We stressed the importance of a consensus between members of staff, but we indicated that it makes sense to include parents in processes of consensus building. We would suggest that parent involvement is a general quality criterion. Consequently parents should participate in such processes. To clarify this position, and to show what it means, we introduced a strategic model, the consensus model. The model represents notions on conditions and processes for finding out what are important goals for a centre are and how they can be justified.

The consensus model, although in current Dutch and other West European practices mainly concerns staff and parents, in principle is relevant to all groups that are, or want to be, responsible for children's centre based education.

The consensus model doesn't exclude the possibility that people will reach a consensus about something that eventually will appear to be bad for children and bad for society. Even if, for instance, social scientists in education or developmental psychology could predict that goals and measures preferred by parents and staff eventually would not be good for children, this won't change the notion that, at least in the present situation, it are the parents' and staff's goals and means that define effective quality in child care.

8 Improving the Quality of ECCE and Multicultural Education

In the preceding two chapters, we presented an evaluative framework for multicultural education in nurseries and playgroups. This is not a simple set of rules or standards that can be used as an absolute measure of quality. Such an absolute measure doesn't exist. It has to be defined and justified repetitively. Particular practices may be effective practices in some centres, whereas comparable practices may be assessed as negatively contributing to the quality of education in other centres. The eventual evaluation depends on the goals that centres themselves want to achieve.

In the Netherlands, as in many Western countries, the definition and selection of educational goals is primarily the responsibility of staff and parents. This means also that there is no single 'best' answer to our main question: How to improve ECCE and multicultural education in ECCE? We, the authors, cannot answer this question by conducting a study and presenting the results in a book, without becoming involved in consensus building with centre staff and parents. We have tried to contribute to the debate by formulating some conditions that are important for improving the quality in centres in Western countries, and identifying activities or measures necessary to meet such conditions. They will now be formulated as recommendations or guidelines. Many are important for consensus building between parents and staff. The recommendations follow from the discussion of the four descriptive models, the three conditions for implementing the consensus model, the consensus model itself and the notion of detours as a strategic means for implementing multicultural education.

The Four Descriptive Models for Multicultural Education

We described ECCE in Dutch nurseries and playgroups and depicted the structure and content in multicultural education. We analysed multicultural education in these centres in terms of goals and means characteristic for four models of multicultural education:

(1) submersion in mainstream language and culture;
(2) a facilitation of the transition between home culture and mainstream culture and language;
(3) changing the mainstream culture and language use within the centre;
(4) influencing ethnic relationships (varying from mutual understanding between people to the prevention of institutional racism).

Our analyses lead to the following general conclusion: between and within centres around Western Europe there is a problem in defining multicultural education in terms of goals and means. There seems some consensus about important goals, but these are rather vague and don't lead to clear ideas about the means (cf. Veen & Vermeulen, 1993). Most centre practices we analysed are best described by a combination of models. This need not be problematic except when it concerns a combination of Model 1 with either Model 2 or 3. These models don't fit comfortably together. However, we found some centres containing these problematic combinations. It seemed that these centres left the choice of activities and materials too much to the responsibility of individual caregivers.

Another problem concerns the situation in which a centre preaches the importance of particular goals, without using the necessary means to achieve the goals. These centres lack a clear, consistent pedagogical approach.

If, as we stated, the quality of ECCE and multicultural education can only be assessed by the extent to which goals are being realised, this means that our analyses of centres in terms of the models lead to at least three quality criteria:

- Centres may combine goals and means characteristic of Models 2, 3, and 4, but the goals typical of Models 2 and 3 cannot be combined with goals and means characteristic of Model 1.
- Goals and means in a centre must be consistent with each other.
- All caregivers in a centre should work towards achieving the same goals. Not doing this means that goal achievement is impaired.

Recommendations

(1) Developing and discussing a clear and consistent pedagogical plan with the whole team is an important means to comply with these criteria and to improve the quality of education, including multicultural education, in a centre.

(2) Goals should be sufficiently clear and concrete to allow for 'translation' into means.

(3) The eventual curriculum should be well structured, but tuned to children's developmental needs. For young children to be able to accommodate appropriate developmental opportunities, a well structured curriculum can be of great help. Structured curricula do not necessarily restrict children's initiative and self-regulation. They give children a solid foundation and a recognition of activity patterns and opportunities for choice.

Three Conditions for Consensus

The four descriptive models may be helpful in defining the preferred quality of a centre, but they don't justify educational goals and means. We have showed that staff almost exclusively define and justify the quality of preschool education in general, and multicultural education in particular. We clarified that a well functioning consensus process involving staff and parents is important for defining and justifying the quality of preschool education.

Apart from the four descriptive models and the strategic model, we identified three important conditions for consensus building which, at the same time, are important ingredients for good quality multicultural education. These three conditions (anti-discrimination, family involvement and responsivity) are closely interrelated. They support each other, but at the same time they presuppose each other. For all three, however, it is clear that using them correctly, requires intensive (partly self organised) study or training. This is exemplified in the notion of responsivity. We consider responsivity to be of permanent importance to quality education, irrespective of which model of multicultural education is adopted.

Responsivity, however, is difficult to achieve. Responsivity and ethnocentrism don't fit together. Since everybody has to deal with a portion of ethnocentrism due to a restricted knowledge of the broad cultural variety of people in society (and due to personal value preferences), it is difficult for staff to be responsive in all educational situations. The need for responsivity in caregivers is a prerequisite for children and parents to feel at ease and welcome in the centre and to flourish. Responsivity requires self reflection on staff values and in-service education in order to be able and willing to be responsive with children and parents from a variety of cultural backgrounds (cf. Banks, 1986).

A short description of three goals that should be central to such learning or training is now provided. They are adapted versions of goals of the curriculum of the Sophie Scholl College in Duisburg (Germany). Iris Taubert, a teacher at this college, gave us a short description of the College's curriculum and the goals, which in turn provide *recommendations* for improvement.

(1) Students have to become aware of their own unavoidable ethno-centrism; how this reveals itself, when, why, and what to do about it?

(2) Problems in everyday live between persons from different cultural backgrounds should be identified. These problems mainly arise from cultural differences in interpretation of situations and messages. These differences need to be explored and coded in ways that allow for better understanding.

(3) Students have to learn to deal with feelings of displeasure and fear linked to cultural strangeness. These feelings should be re-oriented to become curiosity about the unknown. Students, moreover, should learn to be tolerant when parts of a strange culture are contradictory to their own value preferences. They should learn, however, that toler-ance is an instrument of reason to be controlled by themselves, requiring constant reflection of decisions that justify its use. No contradiction should be tolerated. For instance, one should not automatically accept any preference for gender roles. Students have to find out what are their limits of tolerance, and where these are based on.

The Consensus Model

Education in multicultural settings should constitute a continuing process of communication about mutually agreed educational goals and means, preferably between persons from a variety of cultural backgrounds. Limiting the practice of the consensus model to culturally homogeneous groups, which is a real possibility within the context of relative autonomy, could easily lead to the founding of educational institutions along ethnic, political or religious lines. As a step towards further emancipation of particular ethnic minority groups and a future commitment to attempts to break culture and language barriers in a society, this might be a respectable temporary practice. If, however, it leads to further cultural isolation and segregation, this practice might be a step away from mutual understanding and peaceful coexistence.

Bringing persons together who own different values or who value the same values differently, can only lead to consensus if they are committed to common values as well. Participants in the discourse preferably support a notion of mild cultural relativism and cultural transformation. This means that, for the good of a consensus, participants accept that some values will have a different impact in educational practice than they individually would have preferred, or even that new values are defined as common ground based on different value preferences. Consensus formation in such a setting would be a genuine process of value education.

From other studies (Eldering & Vedder, 1992; Van Dijke, Terpstra & Hermanns, 1994) we know that for a variety of reasons, ranging from confidence in the quality of the centre, to limited language proficiency, to protection of one's own feelings of respect and self esteem, ethnic minority parents have more problems in communicating about their children's education with centre staff than Dutch parents. Practising the consensus model in Dutch multicultural society would imply that caregivers reach out to invite and support ethnic minority parents to participate. This might mean that, as a temporary measure, centres organise special meetings for Moroccan mothers or for fathers only. Reaching out to parents is not an easy matter. There are needs and dilemmas that must be addressed if a realignment of parent–professional relations is to be realised. A major challenge is to define in clear operational terms the competencies and behaviours that are indigenous to professionals working with families (Powell, 1988).

Recommendations

Centre staff might take the following steps to enable parents to communicate their educational wishes and needs:

(1) Make sure that parents feel welcome in the centre and that they know that there is always a member of staff available to speak with them.

(2) If parents have enough time to get used to the centre routine (and when they are acquainted with some staff members), the centre may use a more active approach. They may ask parents whether the child enjoys the centre, whether attending the centre has changed the child's language competences, whether they have ideas about what kind of food, activities or type of attention would be good for the child, or would make the child's stay in the centre more enjoyable .

(3) Staff might adopt a rule that if they don't know how to handle a child, or how to grasp a child's attention, they could start to locate a solution by asking parents what they think might be the best strategy. Implementing such a rule eventually leads to a clear picture of the educational wishes and needs of children and their parents.

(4) When all these steps have been taken, staff can start more formal discussions with parents directed at consensus building.

The consensus model allows centres to combine defining important goals for ECCE with finding justification for these goals and support for implementing them. Defining and justifying goals are important for accountability. Accountability in ECCE refers to the notion that centres are held responsible for what they achieve and fail to achieve. Most centres in the Netherlands, are accountable to their communities in matters of safety and hygiene. As regards the pedagogical quality, however, they are primarily accountable to parents, since so far in the Netherlands, other organisations did not want (national administration) or did not succeed in gaining an influential power position (e.g. committees on the quality of ECCE).

As indicated in Chapters 3 and 4, many parents don't fulfil their task to safeguard the pedagogical quality of centres. This is due to several reasons, which we have referred to in preceding chapters. An important reason is the shortage of places in child-care centres. Parents are often glad to find a place where they can leave their children while they are working. They therefore do not wish to be too critical. Van Dijke, Terpstra & Hermanns (1994) suggest that some parents cope with this potentially unsatisfactory situation by avoiding thinking about the possible negative aspects of this situation. They cannot afford to think that their children are not in a developmentally enriching situation. The thought would make their decision to follow a professional career or to earn a living more stressful than it is. Another important reason is that institutional child care has a tradition of strong autonomy, justified by the notion of the professional who knows what is best for children compared with non-professional parents, and also by the notion that some parents are not fit to properly educate their children. As a consequence professionals have rarely felt accountable to parents, and contacts between parents and professionals have been minimal (cf. Singer, 1992).

This situation is, however, changing, although it still holds for many immigrant parents. In our interviews, we heard more than once that immigrant parents think that caregivers know what is best for their children, or in the words of one of the interviewees: 'Parents do see us as professionals. Some don't dare talk to us and would certainly say nothing that might be understood as a directive'.

A third reason is that it is difficult to make clear statements about the quality of centre care. This book is proof of this. As long as parents are seen as, or behave as individual consumers of centre care mainly interested in the good of their child, individual wishes will have to be weighed against the general good of the group. Centre care deals with individual children, but in a group context that cannot always cater for a broad range of different individual wishes.

The consensus model provides a solution to this latter problem, but it cannot function unless the impact of the first two reasons decreases.

Recommendations

(1) Communities should provide sufficient places in ECCE centres that are available for parents and their children irrespective of their income or employment situation.

(2) As regards staff's and parents' mutual responsibility for children's education, professional caregivers should avoid putting up a shield of professionalism, hampering communication between parents and staff.

Diversions to a Better Future

We have discussed key issues in this and preceding chapters. Is mother tongue tuition the best route to success in learning and gaining proficiency in a second language, or is it an unnecessary diversion and a waste of time? Should centre staff organise meetings for Moroccan women or does this lead away from the goal of greater social involvement and participation in public functions and institutions? Is the founding of Islamic, Roman Catholic and West Indian centres proof of a failing multicultural educational policy or just another route to a more multicultural society? We contrasted educational strategies for all children (general strategies) with strategies meant especially for ethnic minority children (particularistic strategies). Both types should contribute to an improvement in the quality of life for all members of a multicultural society. Whether, particularistic strategies will have this function is difficult to say. It will depend on how the 'attending' ethnic minority children and parents as well as the non-attending other children and parents will respond. Envy and a growing disenchantment are routes for the best laid plans and policies to lead to dead-end alleys.

Appendix 1:
Experts Participating in the Workshop on Multicultural Education in Child-Care Institutions

Josette Combes

Since 1986, she has been one of the key influences in developing the Association des Collectifs Enfants Parents Professionels (ACEPP), a French non-governmental umbrella organisation based in Paris, which provides technical support, advice, training and advocacy for parents and professionals wishing to set up community day care centres. Trained as a socio-linguist with experience of working with adolescents and adults, she has had particular responsibility within the ACEPP for developing parent controlled centres in disadvantaged areas. As such she is also coordinator of the Bernard van Leer supported project, based within ACEPP to develop such centres in multicultural communities.

Roel Copier

Born in Rotterdam in 1947 Roel started as a ship sales broker in 1967. In 1979 he started the teachers training school in Delft, which he successfully concluded in 1984 as a teacher in History and English. Since 1991 he has been project-coordinator of Stichting De Meeuw in Rotterdam for Samenspel Rotterdam. In this project immigrant families with young children are encouraged to attend playgroups by organising afternoon playgroups ('spelmiddagen'), where both the child and the mother are invited. He is also author of the manual about how to organize and integrate these afternoon playgroups into existing day care provisions.

Rieke Evegroen

Born in 1947 in Rotterdam, The Netherlands. She studied Educational Studies at the University of Amsterdam. She worked for five years at the Foundation Four Cities project, a foundation in which the four largest cities in Holland work together to prevent educational disadvantages. She was responsible for projects and programme development for nurseries and playgroups. Presently she is working at the Averroès Foundation, a foundation responsible for the development and nation wide implementation of educational intervention programmes for young children and their parents.

Willem Fase

Willem Fase teaches sociology, particularly sociology of education, at Erasmus University Rotterdam, The Netherlands. The major part of his publications concern education and ethnicity. Main topics are theory and practice of intercultural education, international comparisons of policy answers to multilingualism, ethnic claims on the Dutch public/private education debate, transition from school to work for young migrants in Holland. In January 1994 he published another book on comparative analysis of education and ethnicity, entitled *Ethnic Divisions in Western European Education*.

Henriette Heimgaertner

Studied History, Political Science, Geography in Mainz and Heidelberg (Germany), and Gender and Developmental Studies in The Hague (The Netherlands). She was a teacher in Germany, Italy, and Ghana. She developed curricula for and trained development workers in The Netherlands and Germany and worked for an integrated rural development project in Mali. In 1990 she joined the Bernard van Leer Foundation as a programme specialist responsible for project appraisal, monitoring and programme development within the European region (Germany, France, Italy, Greece, Sweden and Norway).

Hetty Kook

Born in 1956 in Willemstad (on the island Curaçao of the Netherlands Antilles). In 1983 she received her degree in Educational Studies at the University of Groningen. Since then she has worked as a researcher and curriculum developer at the Department of Education in Curaçao, as a coordinator of educational issues at the National Platform of Antillean

Organisations, as teacher Papiamento, and as researcher at the University of Amsterdam. Among other things she has been involved in the development of a curriculum for the education of infants (age 4–6). In 1994 she finished her PhD dissertation on the development of reading and writing skills in young bilingual children.

Heleen Langerwerf

Received her training as a teacher, and specialized in working with learning disabled children and organization policy and management. Now she is working as a director at an intercultural nursery ('Hannie Schaft Centrum' in Haarlem, The Netherlands). This nursery works with Dutch and Turkish children and teachers, and uses a bilingual multicultural working method.

Griet Lommez

Studied adult education and worked since 1978 for many years as a social worker in Berchem, near Antwerp in Belgium. Since 1992 she is a manager of an educational centre in Berchem combining a playgroup and a centre for adult education for low qualified, unemployed women. Many of these are migrants.

Edward C. Melhuish

From 1986 to 1971 Edward C. Melhuish studied Psychology at the University of Bristol, Great Britain. Since 1989 he has been the director of the Child Study Centre, Psychology Department, University of Wales, Bangor. His research interests are in social and cognitive development in early childhood; child care; parenting; child development and social policy. He is particularly interested in longitudinal studies. He has produced several books and articles, such as *Day Care for Young Children: International Perspectives* (1991, co-editor, P. Moss), 'Socio-emotional behaviour at 18 months as a function of day care experience, temperament and gender' (1987, in *Infant Mental Health Journal*, 4), 'Type of child care at 18 months: Relations with cognitive and language development' (1990, in *Journal of Child Psychology and Psychiatry*, 12), 'How similar are day care groups before the start of day care' (1991, in *Journal of Applied Developmental Psychology*, 12).

Els Ranshuysen

Has studied Adult Education at the University of Utrecht, The Netherlands. Now she is working at the National Training Body for the

Apprenticeship system that covers the sector of 'Personal and Social Services and Health Care'. She coordinates the vocational training for child care teachers. That means that she is responsible for the innovation and for the guarding of quality of this vocational training course at national level.

Liesbeth Schreuder

Born in 1949 in Amsterdam, The Netherlands. She studied Psychology at the University of Amsterdam. From 1983 till 1993 she worked in an institute concerned with information, advice, training and innovation on behalf of child care centres in Amsterdam. Since February 1993 she has been working at the Dutch Institute for Care and Welfare (NIZW). This is a national institute responsible for research and development on behalf of welfare services, among which child care centres.

Marja van den Sigtenhorst

Was born in 1950. After three years of studying law she has finished a study in adult education and women studies. Since 1991 she is the director of the Centre for Science and Research of Leiden University. Centres for Science and Research form a practical and effective bridge between science and society. Started at the end of the seventies, these centres are now an integral, undisputed part of the Dutch university structure. The main tasks are research-mediation and advising. The research project, 'Multicultural Education in Child-Care Centres in The Netherlands' is one of the projects that has been initiated and partly financed by the Centre for Science and Research of Leiden University.

Elly Singer

Elly Singer (born 1948) studied pedagogy and psychology. Now she is a researcher and lecturer at the Universities of Utrecht and Amsterdam, The Netherlands. She has experience in education and child care and has undertaken many studies on the psychology of parenthood, child rearing practices and provision, and professional intervention in problem situations. Her work contains both studies at a historical and theoretical level (for instance *Child Care and the Psychology of Development*, Routledge 1992) and studies at a practical level (for instance for the Department of Welfare, Health and Culture on the quality of day care centres and the position of parents). She was a member of the committee on the quality of day care provisions (Commissie Kwaliteit Kinderopvang) by government order.

Iram Siraj-Blatchford

Is senior lecturer in Early Childhood Education at the University of London. She has taught in nursery, infant and primary schools and has been involved in teacher education for the past eight years. Her research interests include teacher education and racial equality; quality and equality in combined pre-school provisions and in infant schools; and the development of appropriate research methodology and epistemology to investigate issues of social justice. Her publications include *Race, Gender and Education of Teachers* (1993, Open University Press); *The Early Years: Laying the Foundations for Racial Equality* (1993) and *Effective Teaching in the Early Years: Fostering Children's Learning in Nurseries and Infant Classes* (co-authored, 1992) both by Trentham Books. Currently she is engaged in two funded research projects, one on 'Nursery Centres Meeting Community Needs and Quality in Children's Learning' and the other on 'Racial Equality in Initial Teacher Education'.

Monica Springer-Geldmacher

In the 1970s she received her Master of Art in Educational Science at the University of Essen, Germany. She undertook research at the University of Essen on integration of children with disabilities within the regular school system. From 1981 to 1986 she has been Head of the RAA Gelsenkirchen (Regional Office for the support of migrant children, youth and their parents). She was also engaged in the realization of Community Education and Intercultural Education within the regular school system, and in the installation of special pre-school groups for migrant children and their mothers. From 1987 until today she is a member of the General Office for the RAA (16 regional Offices within Northrhine-Westphalia).

Rita Swinnen

Was trained in the early seventies as a psychologist at the State University of Gent, Belgium. In 1986 she joined the Bernard van Leer Foundation as a programme specialist, responsible for project appraisal, project monitoring and programme development within the European and Mediterranean Region (in particular for the following countries: Belgium, Egypt, The Netherlands, Morocco and Turkey).

Iris Taubert-Kittmann

Was born in 1956 in Duisburg (Germany). She studied Education and German as a Second Language at the Ruhr University in Bochum. Since 1985 she has been teaching the subjects German, Pedagogy, Sociology, and

Psychology and didactics at the Sophie-Scholl-Kollegschule in Duisburg, a teacher training college for a.o. nursery and kindergarten teachers.

Ignasi Vila

A lecturer at the University of Barcelona and has been Director of the Institute of Educational Sciences at this university, as well as Secretary of the Educational Sciences Division. He has carried out substantial research on language acquisition, especially in the area of simultaneous acquisition of two languages, and on the relationship between development and learning from a Vygotskian perspective. Currently he is in charge of the Context Infancy programme, supported by the Barcelona Local Authority and the Bernard van Leer Foundation. The aim is the development of a global model of services to infants in the city of Barcelona.

The Organisers

Ellen Bouwer

Ellen Bouwer was born in 1965 in Rotterdam (The Netherlands). In 1990 she finished her study Psychology at the University of Utrecht. She is a researcher at the University of Leiden in the Centre for Intercultural Pedagogics. Currently she is studyig the relation between cultural orientation in migrant parents and their children's school career.

Marijke Hamel

Marijke Hamel was born in Breda (in the south of The Netherlands) and studied Sociology of Non-Western Societies at the University of Leiden. Specialized in the sociology of education and the regions Latin America and the Caribbean. She is a research assistant at the Centre for Intercultural Pedagogics at Leiden University.

Trees Pels

Born in 1950 in Amsterdam, The Netherlands. Since 1977 she has worked as a scientific secretary and researcher for several institutions. In 1991 she received her doctor's degree at Leiden University on a study of the cultural heritage of Moroccan infants. Her research interests lie in subjects as the socialisation and development of ethnic minority children, preschool education and education outside school. Since 1993 she has been working as a senior researcher at the Erasmus University Rotterdam.

Paul Vedder

Paul Vedder was born on 3 May 1955 in a small village in the northern part of The Netherlands. Since 1991 he is a lecturer and senior researcher at the Centre for Intercultural Pedagogics of Leiden University. He is working on studies on home intervention programmes in ethnic minority families, multicultural education, and the education and learning of Antillian children.

References

Aboud, F.E. (1987) The development of ethnic self-identification and attitudes. In J.S. Phinney and M.J. Rotheram (eds) *Children's Ethnic Socialization: Puralism and Development*. Newbury Park, CA: Sage.

Allport, G.W. (1979) *The Nature of Prejudice*. Cambridge, MA: Addison-Wesley.

Beutler, K. (1969) Aspects of an educational learning theory. *Review of Educational Research* 60, 603–624.

Bidney, D. (1953) The concept of culture and some cultural fallacies. In D. Bidney (ed.) *Theoretical Anthropology*. New York: Columbia University Press.

Bohnsack, F. and Rückriem, G. (1969) *Pädagogische Autonomie und gesellschaftlicher Fortschrittstrukturen und Probleme der Zielsetzung und Eigenständigkeit der Erziehung*. Weinheim: Beltz.

Bowman, B. (1991) Educating language minority children: Challenges and opportunities. In Sharon Lynn Kagan (ed.) *The Care and Education of America's Young Children: Obstacles and Opportunities*. Chicago: University of Chicago Press.

Bruner, J. (1980) *Under Five in Britain*. London: Grant, McIntyre.

CBS (1992) *Niet-Nederlanders in Nederland*. Voorburg/Heerlen: Centraal Bureau voor de Statistiek.

— (1993) *Kindercentra 1992*. Voorburg/Heerlen: Centraal Bureau voor de Statistiek.

Clarke-Stewart, K.A. (1991) A home is not a school: The effects of child care on children's development. *Journal of Social Issues* 47, 105–123.

— (1993) *Daycare*. Revised edition. Cambridge: Harvard University Press.

Clarke-Stewart, K.A. and Fein, G.G. (1983) Early childhood programs. In M.M. Haith and J.J. Campos (eds) *Handbook of Child Psychology, Vol. 2: Infancy and Developmental Psychobiology*. New York: Wiley.

Clerkx, L.E. (1985) Vermaatschappelijking of privatisering van de kinderopvang, de rol van de staat ten aanzien van de emancipatie van vrouwen en kinderen. *Sociaal-Feministische Teksten* 9, 71–91.

— (1990) De belangen van moeders en kinderen, kinderopvang en klasseverhoudingen in Nederland. *Vernieuwing* 49, 3–6.

Clerkx, L. E. and, van IJzendoorn, M.H. (1992) Child care in a Dutch context: On the history, current status, and evaluation of nonmaternal child care in the Netherlands. In M.E. Lamb, K.J. Sternberg, C-P. Hwang and A.G. Broberg (eds) *Child Care in Context. Cross-Cultural Perspectives*. Hillsdale, NJ: Lawrence Erlbaum Associates Inc.

Coleman, P. and Collinge, J. (1991) In the web: Internal and external influences affecting school improvement. *School Effectiveness and School Improvement* 2, 262–285.

Commissie Allochtone Leerlingen in het Onderwijs (1992) *Ceders in de tuin. Naar een nieuwe opzet van het onderwijsbeleid van allochtone leerlingen*. Zoetermeer: Ministerie van Onderwijs en Wetenschappen.

Commissie Kwaliteit Kinderopvang (1994) *De kunst van de kinderopvang*. Utrecht: SWP.

Cummins, J. (1990) Multilingual/multicultural education: Evaluation of underlying theoretical constructs and consequences for curriculum development. In P. Vedder (ed.) *Fundamental Studies in Educational Research*. Amsterdam: Swets and Zeitlinger.

Cziko, G.A. (1992) The evaluation of bilingual education. *Educational Researcher* 21 (2), 10–15.

Dickinson, D. (1993) Features of early childhood environments that support development of language and literacy. In J. Duchan, R. Sonnenmeier and L. Hewitt (eds) *Pragmatics: From Theory to Practice*. Englewood Cliffs, NJ: Prentice Hall.

Duyme, M. (1988) School success and social class; An adoption study. *Developmental Psychology* 24, 203–209.

Eldering, L. (1993) Cultuurverschillen in een multiculturele samenleving. *Comenius* 49, 9–26.

Eldering, L. and Kloprogge, J. (eds) 1989) *Different Cultures Same School. Ethnic Minority Children in Europe*. Amsterdam/Lisse: Swets and Zeitlinger.

Eldering L. and Leseman, P. (eds) (1993) *Early Intervention and Culture*. Paris: UNESCO.

Eldering, L. and Vedder, P. (1992) *OPSTAP: Een opstap naar meer schoolsucces?* Amsterdam/Lisse: Swets and Zeitlinger.

Entzinger, H.B. and Stijnen, P.J.J. (eds) (1990) *Etnische minderheden in Nederland*. Meppel/Amsterdam: Boom/Heerlen: Open Universiteit.

Epstein, A.L. (1978) *Ethos and Ethnicity: Three Studies in Ethnicity*. London: Tavistock Publications.

Extra, G. and Verhoeven, L. (1993) *Community Languages in The Netherlands*. Amsterdam: Swets and Zeitlinger.

Fase, W. (1990) Maatschappelijke achtergronden van de verdeling van etnische groepen in het scholenveld. *Migrantenstudies* 6 (2), 17–30.

Fase, W., Kole, S.C.A., van Paridon, C.A.G.M. and Vlug, V. (1990) *Vorm geven aan intercultureel onderwijs*. De Lier: Academic Book Centre.

Fase, W. and van den Berg, G. (1985) *Theorie en praktijk van intercultureel onderwijs*. Rotterdam: SVO/EUR.

Foucault, M. (1980) *Power-Knowledge: Selected Interviews and Other Writings, 1972–1977*. Brighton: Harvester Press.

Harkness, S. and Super, Ch. (1993) The developmental niche: Implications for children's literacy development. In L. Eldering and P. Leseman (eds) *Early Intervention and Culture*. Paris: UNESCO.

Hewstone, M. (1989) Intergoup attribution: Some implications for the study of ethnic prejudice. In J.P. van Oudenhoven and T.M. Willemsen (eds) *Ethnic Minorities*. Amsterdam: Swets and Zeitlinger.

Heydorn, H.J. (1970) *Über den Widerspruch von Bildung und Herrschaft*. Frankfurt am Main: Europaïsche Verlaganstalt.

Hofstede, G. (1989) Empirical models of cultural differences. Address to the Second Regional Conference of the International Association for Cross-Cultural Psychology, Amsterdam.

Hofstede, G. (1991) *Cultures and Organizations: Software of the Mind*. London: McGraw-Hill.

Hopman, M. (1990) Gehechtheidsrelatie stelt hoge eisen aan crecheleidster. *Kinderopvang* 9, 5–7.

Howes, C. and Hamilton, C.E. (1993) The changing experience of child care: Changes in teachers and in teacher–child relationships and children's social competence with peers. *Early Childhood Research Quarterly* 8, 15–32.

Huisken, F. (1974) *Zur Kritik bürgerlicher Didaktik und Bildungsökonomie*. München: List Verlag.

Jap-a-Joe, S. and Leseman, P. (1994) *Hindostaanse gezinnen*. Amsterdam: SCO-Kohnstamm instituut.

Kagitçibasi, Ç. (1987) Individual and group loyalties, are they compatible? In Kagitçibasi, Ç. (ed.) *Growth and Progress in Cross-cultural Psychology*. Berwyn/Lisse: Swets and Zeitlinger.

— (1989) Child rearing in Turkey. Implications for immigration and intervention. In L. Eldering and J. Kloprogge (eds) *Different Cultures, Same School: Ethnic Minority Children in Europe*. Amsterdam: Swets and Zeitlinger.

Klafki, W. (1963) *Studien zur Bildungstheorie und Didaktik*. Weinheim: Beltz.

Köksal, A. and Van der Wal, R. (1990) *Stichting Samenspel Rotterdam*. Rotterdam: Stichting Samenspel.

Kook, H. and Vedder, P. (1994) Tweetaligheid en taalstimulering thuis. In T. Pels (ed.) *De ontwikkeling tot 12 jaar; mogelijkheden voor interventie bij allochtone kinderen*. Leiden: Leiden University/PEWA.

Kroeber, A. and Kluckhon, C. (1952) *Culture: A Critical Review of Concepts and Definitions*. Cambridge, MA: Harvard University Press.

Lee, H. (1992) Day care in the People's Republic of China. In M.E. Lamb, K.J. Sternberg, C-P. Hwang and A.G. Broberg (eds) *Child Care in Context. Cross-cultural Perspectives*. Hillsdale, NJ: Lawrence Erlbaum Associates Inc.

Leseman, P.P.M. (1989) *Structurele en pedagogische determinanten van schoolloopbanen*. Rotterdam: Rotterdamse Schooladviesdienst.

— (1994) Preventie van leermoeilijkheden en onderwijsachterstand. In J. Rispens, H. Groenendaal and P. Goudena (eds) *Van kindmodel naar modelkind*. Groningen: Stichting Kinderstudies.

Lucassen, L. and Köbben, A. (1992) *Het partiële gelijk*. Amsterdam: Swets and Zeitlinger.

Lundgren, U. (1983) Curriculum development and educational quality. In B. Creemers, W. Hoeben and K. Koops (eds) *De kwaliteit van het onderwijs*. Groningen: Wolters Noordhoff.

McLaughlin, B. (1987) Reading in a second language: Studies with adult and child learners. In S. Goldman and H. Trueba (eds) *Becoming Literate in English as a Second Language*. Norwood, NJ: Ablex.

McLaughlin, M. (1987) Learning from experience: Lessons from policy implementation. *Educational Evaluation and Policy Analysis* 9, 171–178.

Melhuish, E. (1993) Preschool care and education: Lessons from the 20th for the 21st century. *International Journal of Early Years Education* 1 (2), 19–32.

Melhuish, E. and Moss, P. (eds) (1991) *Day Care for Young Children, International Perspectives*. London, New York: Tavistock/Routledge.

Milner, D. (1983) *Children and Race: Ten Years On*. London: Ward Lock Educational.

Ministerie van Justitie (1994) *Het Nederlandse vreemdelingenbeleid*. Den Haag: Ministerie van Justitie.

Moll, L. (1992) Bilingual classroom studies and community analysis: Some recent trends. *Educational Researcher* 21, 20–24.

Moll, L. and Greenberg, J. (1990) Creating zones of possibilities. In L. Moll (ed.) *Vygotsky and Education.* Cambridge: Cambridge University Press.

Moss, P. (1988) *Childcare and Equality of Opportunity.* Brussels: Commission of the European Communities.

Mosterd, E. (1992) Maak eerst je pedagogische uitgangspunten zichtbaar. *Kinderopvang* 12, 12–13.

Nohl, H. (1967) *Ausgewählte pädagogische Abhandlungen.* Paderborn: Schönigh.

Ogbu, J. (1992) Understanding cultural diversity and learning. *Educational Researcher* 21, 5–14.

Payne, M.A. and Hinds, J.O. (1986) Parent–teacher relationships: Perspectives from a developing country. *Educational Research* 28, 117–125.

Pels, T. (1991) *Marokkaanse kleuters en hun culturele kapitaal.* Amsterdam: Swets and Zeitlinger.

— (1993) Het belang van het cultuurbeleid in het onderwijs. *Comenius* 49, 42–55.

Pettigrew, T. (1979) The ultimate attribution error. *Personality and Social Psychology Bulletin* 5, 461–476.

POLKA, ontwikkelplan (1989) Rotterdam: Vier Steden Project Welzijn.

Pot, L. (1991) *Kwaliteit van kinderopvang in de steigers.* Utrecht: NIZW.

Powell, D.R. (1989) Challenges in the design and evaluation of parent–child intervention programs. In D.R. Powell (ed.) *Parent Education as Early Childhood Intervention: Emerging Directions in Theory, Research and Practice.* Norwood, NJ: Ablex.

Rabain-Jamain, J. (1989) Pratiques de soin et interaction mère–enfant dans un contexte d'émigration. In J. Retschitzky, M. Bossel-Lagos and P. Dasen (eds) *La recherche interculturelle* Tome 2. Paris: L'Harmattan.

Raikes, H. (1993) Relationship during infant care: Time with a high ability teacher and infant–teacher attachment. *Early Childhood Research Quarterly* 8, 309–325.

Riksen-Walraven, J.M.A. (1992) Instapje: De ontwikkeling van een interventieprogramma voor ouders met kinderen van 12 tot 18 maanden. In J. Rispens and B.F. van der Meulen (eds) *Gezinsgerichte stimulering van kinderen in achterstandssituaties.* Amsterdam/Lisse: Swets and Zeitlinger.

Scarr, S. (1992) Developmental theories for the 1990s: Development and individual differences. *Child Development* 63, 1–19.

Scarr, S. and Kidd, K. (1983) Developmental behavior genetics. In M.M. Haith and J.J. Campos (eds) *Handbook of Child Psychology, 2. Infancy and Development.* New York: Wiley.

Schiess, G. (1973) *Die Diskussion über die Autonomie der Pädagogik.* Weinheim: Beltz.

Secord, P.F. and Backman, C.W. (1974) *Social Psychology.* Tokyo: McGraw- Hill Kogakusha.

SGBO (1991) *Kinderopvang in gemeenten.* 's-Gravenhage: Vereniging Nederlandse Gemeenten.

Siguan, M. (1990) Multilingual and multicultural education, what for? Confronting ends and means. In P. Vedder (ed.) *Fundamental Studies in Educational Research.* Amsterdam: Swets and Zeitlinger.

Singer, E. (1990) Mijn kind heeft een driehoeksverhouding. *Vernieuwing* 49 (1), 7–10.

— (1992) *Child-care and the Psychology of Development.* London: Routledge.

Skolnick, S. (1973) *The Intimate Environment: Exploring Marriage and the Family.* Boston: Little and Brown.

Slavin, R., Karweit, N. and Madden, N. (eds) (1989) *Effective Programs for Students at Risk.* Boston: Allan and Bacon.

Smeyers, P. (1991) Het verlangen naar zekerheid en geborgenheid: enkele wijsgerig-pedagogische beschouwingen over opvoeding en onderwijs in de multiculturele samenleving. *Pedagogisch Tijdschrift* 16, 125–137.

Snow, C. (1993) Linguistic development as related to literacy. In L. Eldering and P. Leseman (eds) *Early Intervention and Culture.* Paris: UNESCO.

Stevenson, H. (1992) *The Learning Gap.* New York: Summit Books .

Stone, M. (1981) *The Education of the Black Child in Britain.* Glasgow: Fontana.

Swieringa, T.A. (1986) *Intercultureel analyse kader ontwikkeling 0–4 jarigen.* Leiden: Research voor Beleid.

Taylor, M. (1991) Values in education: A comment. In I. Barr and H. Hooghoff (eds) *Values, Schooling and Society.* The Hague: CIDREE.

Tennekes, J. (1989) Buitenlandse jongeren en cultuurconflict. Migrantenstudies 5 (4), 24–40.

— (1990) *De onbekende dimensie: Over cultuur, cultuurverschillen en macht.* Leuven/Apeldoorn: Garant.

Troyna, B. and Edwards, V. (1993) *The Educational Needs of a Multiracial Society.* Coventry: Centre for Research in Ethnic Relations.

Troyna, B. and Carrington, B. (1990) *Education, Racism and Reform.* London/New York: Routledge.

Van Ballegooijen, A. (1984) *Werken in kindercentra.* Oosterbeek: Werkgemeenschap Kindercentra in Nederland.

Van Bennekom, J., Mostert, E. and Stegenga, M. (1992) *Leidster en directrice in de kinderopvang. Beroepsuitoefening en taken.* Utrecht: NIZW.

Van den Ende, J. (1993) Wij hebben geen interculturele kinderen. MA thesis, Leiden University/ICP.

Van der Graaf, H. and Hoppe, R. (1989) *Beleid en politiek.* Muiderberg: Coutinho.

Van der Ley, A. (ed.) (1991) *Turkse kinderen in onderwijs en opvoeding.* Amsterdam: V.U. Uitgeverij.

Van der Wal, R. and Copier, R. (1993) *Handboek Samenspel.* Rotterdam: Stichting De Meeuw.

Van Dijke, A., Terpstra, L. and Hermanns, J. (1994) *Ouders over kinderopvang.* Amsterdam: SCO-Kohnstamm Instituut, rapport 349.

Van Geert, P. (1991) A dynamic systems model of cognitive and language growth. *Psychological Review* 98, 1–55.

— (1992a) Vygotsky's dynamic systems. *Comenius* 48, 383–401.

— (1992b) Interventie en de dynamica van de ouder-kind interacties. In T. Vallen (ed.) *OPSTAP onder vuur?* Rijswijk: Ministerie van WVC.

Van Keulen, A. and Kleerekoper, L. (1992) *Mozaïek van culturen. Praktijkboek intercultureel werken in kindercentra.* Utrecht: NIZW.

Van Langen, M. and Jungbluth, J. (1990) *De invloed van sociaal-economische factoren op schoolprestaties van allochtone kinderen.* Lisse: Swets and Zeitlinger.

Van Oudenhoven, P.J. (1989) Improving interethnic relationships: How effective is cooperation? In J.P. van Oudenhoven and T. Willemsen (eds) *Ethnic Minorities.* Amsterdam: Swets and Zeitlinger

Vedder, P. (1992) Measuring the quality of education. In P. Vedder (ed.) *Measuring the Quality of Education*. Amsterdam: Swets and Zeitlinger.

— (1993) *Intercultureel onderwijs vanuit psychologisch perspectief*. Leiden: Leiden University/ICP

— (1994) Global measures of the quality of education. A help to developing countries? *International Review of Education* 40, 5–17.

— (1995) *Antilliaanse kinderen; taal opvoeding en onderwijs op de Antillen en in Nederland*. Utrecht: Jan van Arkel.

Vedder, P., Muysken, P. and Kook, H. (in prep.) Language choice and functional differentiation of languages in bilingual parent–child reading sessions.

Veen, A. and Vermeulen, A. (1993) *Kindercentra en meertaligheid*. Amsterdam: SCO-Kohnstamm instituut.

Vermeulen, H. (1992) De cultura. Een verhandeling over het cultuurbegrip in de studie van allochtone etnische groepen. *Migrantenstudies* 8, 14–30.

VNG (1991) *Gemeenten en kinderopvang. Modelverordening*. [Groene reeks 110]. 's-Gravenhage: VNG.

VSP-W (1992a) *POLKA. Een interetnische visie en houding, achtergrondinformatie*. Rotterdam/Amsterdam/Utrecht/Den Haag: VSP-Welzijn.

— (1992b) *Kindercentra en meertaligheid. Voortgangsverslag en Werkplan*. Rotterdam/Amsterdam/Utrecht/Den Haag: VSP-Welzijn.

Weikart, D.P. (1987) Curriculum quality in early education. In S.L. Kagan and E.F. Zigler (eds) *Early Schooling. The National Debate*. New Haven: Yale University Press.

Wertsch, J. (1979) From social interaction to higher psychological processes. *Human Development* 22, 1–22.

Index